Social Data
Complete Self-Assessment Guide

Table of Contents

About The Art of Service   7

Included Resources - how to access   7
Purpose of this Self-Assessment   9
How to use the Self-Assessment   10
Social Data
Scorecard Example   12

Social Data
Scorecard   13

BEGINNING OF THE
SELF-ASSESSMENT: 14
CRITERION #1: RECOGNIZE   15

CRITERION #2: DEFINE: 27

CRITERION #3: MEASURE: 43

CRITERION #4: ANALYZE: 57

CRITERION #5: IMPROVE: 73

CRITERION #6: CONTROL: 88

CRITERION #7: SUSTAIN: 100
Social Data and Managing Projects, Criteria for Project
Managers: 124
1.0 Initiating Process Group: Social Data   125

1.1 Project Charter: Social Data   127

1.2 Stakeholder Register: Social Data   129

1.3 Stakeholder Analysis Matrix: Social Data   130

2.0 Planning Process Group: Social Data   132

2.1 Project Management Plan: Social Data   134

2.2 Scope Management Plan: Social Data   136

2.3 Requirements Management Plan: Social Data   138

2.4 Requirements Documentation: Social Data   140

2.5 Requirements Traceability Matrix: Social Data   142

2.6 Project Scope Statement: Social Data   144

2.7 Assumption and Constraint Log: Social Data   146

2.8 Work Breakdown Structure: Social Data   148

2.9 WBS Dictionary: Social Data   150

2.10 Schedule Management Plan: Social Data   153

2.11 Activity List: Social Data   155

2.12 Activity Attributes: Social Data   157

2.13 Milestone List: Social Data   159

2.14 Network Diagram: Social Data   161

2.15 Activity Resource Requirements: Social Data   163

2.16 Resource Breakdown Structure: Social Data   165

2.17 Activity Duration Estimates: Social Data   167

2.18 Duration Estimating Worksheet: Social Data   169

2.19 Project Schedule: Social Data   171

2.20 Cost Management Plan: Social Data   173

2.21 Activity Cost Estimates: Social Data   175

2.22 Cost Estimating Worksheet: Social Data   177

2.23 Cost Baseline: Social Data   179

2.24 Quality Management Plan: Social Data   181

2.25 Quality Metrics: Social Data   183

2.26 Process Improvement Plan: Social Data   185

2.27 Responsibility Assignment Matrix: Social Data   187

2.28 Roles and Responsibilities: Social Data   189

2.29 Human Resource Management Plan: Social Data   191

2.30 Communications Management Plan: Social Data   193

2.31 Risk Management Plan: Social Data   195

2.32 Risk Register: Social Data   197

2.33 Probability and Impact Assessment: Social Data   199

2.34 Probability and Impact Matrix: Social Data   201

2.35 Risk Data Sheet: Social Data   203

2.36 Procurement Management Plan: Social Data   205

2.37 Source Selection Criteria: Social Data   207

2.38 Stakeholder Management Plan: Social Data 209

2.39 Change Management Plan: Social Data 211

3.0 Executing Process Group: Social Data 213

3.1 Team Member Status Report: Social Data 215

3.2 Change Request: Social Data 217

3.3 Change Log: Social Data 219

3.4 Decision Log: Social Data 221

3.5 Quality Audit: Social Data 223

3.6 Team Directory: Social Data 225

3.7 Team Operating Agreement: Social Data 227

3.8 Team Performance Assessment: Social Data 229

3.9 Team Member Performance Assessment: Social Data 231

3.10 Issue Log: Social Data 233

4.0 Monitoring and Controlling Process Group: Social Data
234

4.1 Project Performance Report: Social Data 236

4.2 Variance Analysis: Social Data 238

4.3 Earned Value Status: Social Data 240

4.4 Risk Audit: Social Data 242

4.5 Contractor Status Report: Social Data 244

4.6 Formal Acceptance: Social Data   246

5.0 Closing Process Group: Social Data   248

5.1 Procurement Audit: Social Data   250

5.2 Contract Close-Out: Social Data   253

5.3 Project or Phase Close-Out: Social Data   255

5.4 Lessons Learned: Social Data   257
Index   259

About The Art of Service

The Art of Service, Business Process Architects since 2000, is dedicated to helping stakeholders achieve excellence.

Defining, designing, creating, and implementing a process to solve a stakeholders challenge or meet an objective is the most valuable role... In EVERY group, company, organization and department.

Unless you're talking a one-time, single-use project, there should be a process. Whether that process is managed and implemented by humans, AI, or a combination of the two, it needs to be designed by someone with a complex enough perspective to ask the right questions.

Someone capable of asking the right questions and step back and say, 'What are we really trying to accomplish here? And is there a different way to look at it?'

With The Art of Service's Standard Requirements Self-Assessments, we empower people who can do just that — whether their title is marketer, entrepreneur, manager, salesperson, consultant, Business Process Manager, executive assistant, IT Manager, CIO etc... —they are the people who rule the future. They are people who watch the process as it happens, and ask the right questions to make the process work better.

Contact us when you need any support with this Self-Assessment and any help with templates, blue-prints and examples of standard documents you might need:

http://theartofservice.com
service@theartofservice.com

Included Resources - how to access

Included with your purchase of the book is the Social Data

Self-Assessment Spreadsheet Dashboard which contains all questions and Self-Assessment areas and auto-generates insights, graphs, and project RACI planning - all with examples to get you started right away.

How? Simply send an email to
access@theartofservice.com
with this books' title in the subject to get the Social Data Self Assessment Tool right away.

You will receive the following contents with New and Updated specific criteria:

•   The latest quick edition of the book in PDF

•   The latest complete edition of the book in PDF, which criteria correspond to the criteria in...

•   The Self-Assessment Excel Dashboard, and...

•   Example pre-filled Self-Assessment Excel Dashboard to get familiar with results generation

•   In-depth specific Checklists covering the topic

•   Project management checklists and templates to assist with implementation

INCLUDES LIFETIME SELF ASSESSMENT UPDATES

Every self assessment comes with Lifetime Updates and Lifetime Free Updated Books. Lifetime Updates is an industry-first feature which allows you to receive verified self assessment updates, ensuring you always have the most accurate information at your fingertips.

Get it now- you will be glad you did - do it now, before you forget.

Send an email to **access@theartofservice.com** with this books' title in the subject to get the Social Data Self Assessment Tool right away.

Purpose of this Self-Assessment

This Self-Assessment has been developed to improve understanding of the requirements and elements of Social Data, based on best practices and standards in business process architecture, design and quality management.

It is designed to allow for a rapid Self-Assessment to determine how closely existing management practices and procedures correspond to the elements of the Self-Assessment.

The criteria of requirements and elements of Social Data have been rephrased in the format of a Self-Assessment questionnaire, with a seven-criterion scoring system, as explained in this document.

In this format, even with limited background knowledge of Social Data, a manager can quickly review existing operations to determine how they measure up to the standards. This in turn can serve as the starting point of a 'gap analysis' to identify management tools or system elements that might usefully be implemented in the organization to help improve overall performance.

How to use the Self-Assessment

On the following pages are a series of questions to identify to what extent your Social Data initiative is complete in comparison to the requirements set in standards.

To facilitate answering the questions, there is a space in front of each question to enter a score on a scale of '1' to '5'.

1 Strongly Disagree

2 Disagree

3 Neutral

4 Agree

5 Strongly Agree

Read the question and rate it with the following in front of mind:

'In my belief, the answer to this question is clearly defined'.

There are two ways in which you can choose to interpret this statement;
1. how aware are you that the answer to the question is clearly defined
2. for more in-depth analysis you can choose to gather evidence and confirm the answer to the question. This obviously will take more time, most Self-Assessment users opt for the first way to interpret the question and dig deeper later on based on the outcome of the overall Self-Assessment.

A score of '1' would mean that the answer is not clear at all, where a '5' would mean the answer is crystal clear and defined. Leave emtpy when the question is not applicable or you don't want to answer it, you can skip it without affecting your score. Write your score in the space provided.

After you have responded to all the appropriate statements in each section, compute your average score for that section, using the formula provided, and round to the nearest tenth. Then transfer to the corresponding spoke in the Social Data Scorecard on the second next page of the Self-Assessment.

Your completed Social Data Scorecard will give you a clear presentation of which Social Data areas need attention.

Social Data
Scorecard Example

Example of how the finalized Scorecard can look like:

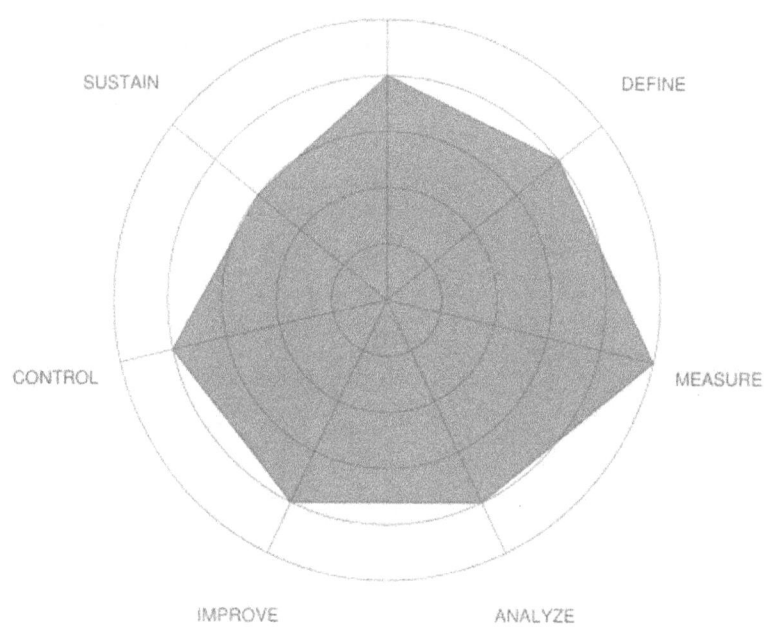

Social Data
Scorecard

Your Scores:

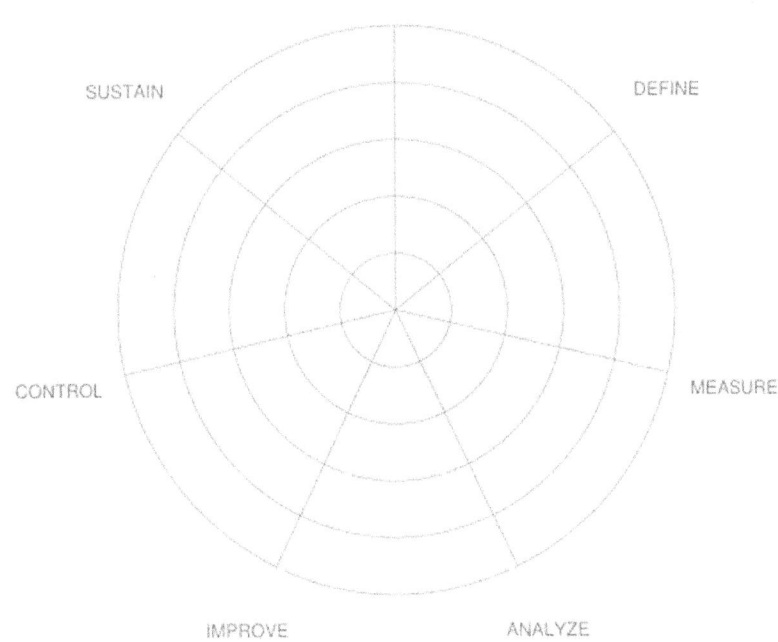

BEGINNING OF THE SELF-ASSESSMENT:

CRITERION #1: RECOGNIZE

INTENT: Be aware of the need for change. Recognize that there is an unfavorable variation, problem or symptom.

In my belief, the answer to this question is clearly defined:

5 Strongly Agree

4 Agree

3 Neutral

2 Disagree

1 Strongly Disagree

1. How do you recognize an objection?
<--- Score

2. Can management personnel recognize the monetary benefit of Social Data?
<--- Score

3. How do you take a forward-looking perspective in identifying Social Data research related to market

response and models?
<--- Score

4. What Social Data problem should be solved?
<--- Score

5. What should be considered when identifying available resources, constraints, and deadlines?
<--- Score

6. How are the Social Data's objectives aligned to the group's overall stakeholder strategy?
<--- Score

7. How do you assess your Social Data workforce capability and capacity needs, including skills, competencies, and staffing levels?
<--- Score

8. Did you miss any major Social Data issues?
<--- Score

9. What training and capacity building actions are needed to implement proposed reforms?
<--- Score

10. What does Social Data success mean to the stakeholders?
<--- Score

11. Are employees recognized or rewarded for performance that demonstrates the highest levels of integrity?
<--- Score

12. Is the quality assurance team identified?

<--- Score

13. Will new equipment/products be required to facilitate Social Data delivery, for example is new software needed?
<--- Score

14. What needs to stay?
<--- Score

15. Who needs to know?
<--- Score

16. Does the problem have ethical dimensions?
<--- Score

17. What are the Social Data resources needed?
<--- Score

18. What situation(s) led to this Social Data Self Assessment?
<--- Score

19. What are your needs in relation to Social Data skills, labor, equipment, and markets?
<--- Score

20. How does it fit into your organizational needs and tasks?
<--- Score

21. What is the problem and/or vulnerability?
<--- Score

22. Are there Social Data problems defined?
<--- Score

23. What is the extent or complexity of the Social Data problem?
<--- Score

24. Are there regulatory / compliance issues?
<--- Score

25. To what extent would your organization benefit from being recognized as a award recipient?
<--- Score

26. Do you need different information or graphics?
<--- Score

27. Do you need to avoid or amend any Social Data activities?
<--- Score

28. How can auditing be a preventative security measure?
<--- Score

29. Where is training needed?
<--- Score

30. What is the recognized need?
<--- Score

31. Will it solve real problems?
<--- Score

32. How are you going to measure success?
<--- Score

33. Are you dealing with any of the same issues today

as yesterday? What can you do about this?
<--- Score

34. Are problem definition and motivation clearly presented?
<--- Score

35. Who needs what information?
<--- Score

36. Does your organization need more Social Data education?
<--- Score

37. What needs to be done?
<--- Score

38. How many trainings, in total, are needed?
<--- Score

39. Who else hopes to benefit from it?
<--- Score

40. Who needs budgets?
<--- Score

41. Think about the people you identified for your Social Data project and the project responsibilities you would assign to them, what kind of training do you think they would need to perform these responsibilities effectively?
<--- Score

42. What are the expected benefits of Social Data to the stakeholder?
<--- Score

43. Why is this needed?
<--- Score

44. Which issues are too important to ignore?
<--- Score

45. What Social Data capabilities do you need?
<--- Score

46. Have you identified your Social Data key performance indicators?
<--- Score

47. Do you have/need 24-hour access to key personnel?
<--- Score

48. How do you recognize an Social Data objection?
<--- Score

49. Are there recognized Social Data problems?
<--- Score

50. What vendors make products that address the Social Data needs?
<--- Score

51. Who needs to know about Social Data?
<--- Score

52. What resources or support might you need?
<--- Score

53. What information do users need?
<--- Score

54. Why the need?
<--- Score

55. What problems are you facing and how do you consider Social Data will circumvent those obstacles?
<--- Score

56. Which information does the Social Data business case need to include?
<--- Score

57. What tools and technologies are needed for a custom Social Data project?
<--- Score

58. Consider your own Social Data project, what types of organizational problems do you think might be causing or affecting your problem, based on the work done so far?
<--- Score

59. Do you recognize Social Data achievements?
<--- Score

60. What is the smallest subset of the problem you can usefully solve?
<--- Score

61. Is it clear when you think of the day ahead of you what activities and tasks you need to complete?
<--- Score

62. What else needs to be measured?
<--- Score

63. Are there any specific expectations or concerns about the Social Data team, Social Data itself?
<--- Score

64. Are employees recognized for desired behaviors?
<--- Score

65. What Social Data coordination do you need?
<--- Score

66. What are the timeframes required to resolve each of the issues/problems?
<--- Score

67. Where do you need to exercise leadership?
<--- Score

68. Are controls defined to recognize and contain problems?
<--- Score

69. Does Social Data create potential expectations in other areas that need to be recognized and considered?
<--- Score

70. What are the clients issues and concerns?
<--- Score

71. Do you know what you need to know about Social Data?
<--- Score

72. What activities does the governance board need to consider?
<--- Score

73. What prevents you from making the changes you know will make you a more effective Social Data leader?
<--- Score

74. Who should resolve the Social Data issues?
<--- Score

75. What would happen if Social Data weren't done?
<--- Score

76. What is the Social Data problem definition? What do you need to resolve?
<--- Score

77. As a sponsor, customer or management, how important is it to meet goals, objectives?
<--- Score

78. Is it needed?
<--- Score

79. Are there any revenue recognition issues?
<--- Score

80. How do you identify the kinds of information that you will need?
<--- Score

81. How are training requirements identified?
<--- Score

82. What is the problem or issue?
<--- Score

83. What do employees need in the short term?
<--- Score

84. To what extent does each concerned units management team recognize Social Data as an effective investment?
<--- Score

85. What extra resources will you need?
<--- Score

86. How much are sponsors, customers, partners, stakeholders involved in Social Data? In other words, what are the risks, if Social Data does not deliver successfully?
<--- Score

87. Who defines the rules in relation to any given issue?
<--- Score

88. What are the minority interests and what amount of minority interests can be recognized?
<--- Score

89. How do you identify subcontractor relationships?
<--- Score

90. Will Social Data deliverables need to be tested and, if so, by whom?
<--- Score

91. Would you recognize a threat from the inside?
<--- Score

92. What do you need to start doing?

<--- Score

93. What creative shifts do you need to take?
<--- Score

94. When a Social Data manager recognizes a problem, what options are available?
<--- Score

95. What are the stakeholder objectives to be achieved with Social Data?
<--- Score

96. What Social Data events should you attend?
<--- Score

97. Is the need for organizational change recognized?
<--- Score

98. Are your goals realistic? Do you need to redefine your problem? Perhaps the problem has changed or maybe you have reached your goal and need to set a new one?
<--- Score

99. Who are your key stakeholders who need to sign off?
<--- Score

Add up total points for this section:
_ _ _ _ _ = Total points for this section

Divided by: _ _ _ _ _ _ (number of statements answered) = _ _ _ _ _ _
Average score for this section

Transfer your score to the Social Data
Index at the beginning of the Self-
Assessment.

CRITERION #2: DEFINE:

INTENT: Formulate the stakeholder problem. Define the problem, needs and objectives.

In my belief, the answer to this question is clearly defined:

5 Strongly Agree

4 Agree

3 Neutral

2 Disagree

1 Strongly Disagree

1. What constraints exist that might impact the team?
<--- Score

2. How have you defined all Social Data requirements first?
<--- Score

3. Are different versions of process maps needed to account for the different types of inputs?

<--- Score

4. How did the Social Data manager receive input to the development of a Social Data improvement plan and the estimated completion dates/times of each activity?
<--- Score

5. What is the scope of Social Data?
<--- Score

6. What are the compelling stakeholder reasons for embarking on Social Data?
<--- Score

7. Is the improvement team aware of the different versions of a process: what they think it is vs. what it actually is vs. what it should be vs. what it could be?
<--- Score

8. What Social Data services do you require?
<--- Score

9. How do you gather Social Data requirements?
<--- Score

10. Has a project plan, Gantt chart, or similar been developed/completed?
<--- Score

11. Has a team charter been developed and communicated?
<--- Score

12. Is the work to date meeting requirements?
<--- Score

13. Is special Social Data user knowledge required?
<--- Score

14. Do you have a Social Data success story or case study ready to tell and share?
<--- Score

15. Has everyone on the team, including the team leaders, been properly trained?
<--- Score

16. What are (control) requirements for Social Data Information?
<--- Score

17. Is there regularly 100% attendance at the team meetings? If not, have appointed substitutes attended to preserve cross-functionality and full representation?
<--- Score

18. Is Social Data currently on schedule according to the plan?
<--- Score

19. Is scope creep really all bad news?
<--- Score

20. Have the customer needs been translated into specific, measurable requirements? How?
<--- Score

21. How are consistent Social Data definitions important?
<--- Score

22. When is the estimated completion date?
<--- Score

23. How would you define Social Data leadership?
<--- Score

24. What are the record-keeping requirements of Social Data activities?
<--- Score

25. Is the current 'as is' process being followed? If not, what are the discrepancies?
<--- Score

26. What are the rough order estimates on cost savings/opportunities that Social Data brings?
<--- Score

27. Do you all define Social Data in the same way?
<--- Score

28. Are stakeholder processes mapped?
<--- Score

29. Is the team equipped with available and reliable resources?
<--- Score

30. Are there different segments of customers?
<--- Score

31. What are the requirements for audit information?
<--- Score

32. Why are you doing Social Data and what is the

scope?
<--- Score

33. Is the Social Data scope manageable?
<--- Score

34. How often are the team meetings?
<--- Score

35. What are the tasks and definitions?
<--- Score

36. Who is gathering Social Data information?
<--- Score

37. What are the core elements of the Social Data business case?
<--- Score

38. Are team charters developed?
<--- Score

39. What would be the goal or target for a Social Data's improvement team?
<--- Score

40. What customer feedback methods were used to solicit their input?
<--- Score

41. What system do you use for gathering Social Data information?
<--- Score

42. Are required metrics defined, what are they?
<--- Score

43. If substitutes have been appointed, have they been briefed on the Social Data goals and received regular communications as to the progress to date?
<--- Score

44. How do you think the partners involved in Social Data would have defined success?
<--- Score

45. How do you manage changes in Social Data requirements?
<--- Score

46. Has the improvement team collected the 'voice of the customer' (obtained feedback – qualitative and quantitative)?
<--- Score

47. What defines best in class?
<--- Score

48. Is full participation by members in regularly held team meetings guaranteed?
<--- Score

49. What information should you gather?
<--- Score

50. What are the Social Data use cases?
<--- Score

51. Do you have organizational privacy requirements?
<--- Score

52. Is there a completed, verified, and validated high-

level 'as is' (not 'should be' or 'could be') stakeholder process map?
<--- Score

53. How do you manage unclear Social Data requirements?
<--- Score

54. How do you hand over Social Data context?
<--- Score

55. In what way can you redefine the criteria of choice clients have in your category in your favor?
<--- Score

56. What is the context?
<--- Score

57. What gets examined?
<--- Score

58. Has anyone else (internal or external to the group) attempted to solve this problem or a similar one before? If so, what knowledge can be leveraged from these previous efforts?
<--- Score

59. Is Social Data required?
<--- Score

60. Is the Social Data scope complete and appropriately sized?
<--- Score

61. How would you define the culture at your organization, how susceptible is it to Social Data

changes?
<--- Score

62. Is the team sponsored by a champion or stakeholder leader?
<--- Score

63. What is the scope of the Social Data work?
<--- Score

64. Is Social Data linked to key stakeholder goals and objectives?
<--- Score

65. Scope of sensitive information?
<--- Score

66. Does the team have regular meetings?
<--- Score

67. What is out of scope?
<--- Score

68. Are roles and responsibilities formally defined?
<--- Score

69. How can the value of Social Data be defined?
<--- Score

70. What are the boundaries of the scope? What is in bounds and what is not? What is the start point? What is the stop point?
<--- Score

71. Is the team adequately staffed with the desired cross-functionality? If not, what additional resources

are available to the team?
<--- Score

72. Has a Social Data requirement not been met?
<--- Score

73. Who approved the Social Data scope?
<--- Score

74. How do you catch Social Data definition inconsistencies?
<--- Score

75. Will team members perform Social Data work when assigned and in a timely fashion?
<--- Score

76. How and when will the baselines be defined?
<--- Score

77. What scope to assess?
<--- Score

78. What Social Data requirements should be gathered?
<--- Score

79. How do you build the right business case?
<--- Score

80. Are all requirements met?
<--- Score

81. What happens if Social Data's scope changes?
<--- Score

82. Who defines (or who defined) the rules and roles?
<--- Score

83. What are the dynamics of the communication plan?
<--- Score

84. What intelligence can you gather?
<--- Score

85. What is the worst case scenario?
<--- Score

86. What was the context?
<--- Score

87. Has a high-level 'as is' process map been completed, verified and validated?
<--- Score

88. Is there a critical path to deliver Social Data results?
<--- Score

89. When is/was the Social Data start date?
<--- Score

90. Do the problem and goal statements meet the SMART criteria (specific, measurable, attainable, relevant, and time-bound)?
<--- Score

91. Has/have the customer(s) been identified?
<--- Score

92. Are there any constraints known that bear on the

ability to perform Social Data work? How is the team addressing them?
<--- Score

93. Is there any additional Social Data definition of success?
<--- Score

94. What critical content must be communicated – who, what, when, where, and how?
<--- Score

95. Does the scope remain the same?
<--- Score

96. Are audit criteria, scope, frequency and methods defined?
<--- Score

97. How is the team tracking and documenting its work?
<--- Score

98. Has your scope been defined?
<--- Score

99. What key stakeholder process output measure(s) does Social Data leverage and how?
<--- Score

100. Are task requirements clearly defined?
<--- Score

101. Are improvement team members fully trained on Social Data?
<--- Score

102. What specifically is the problem? Where does it occur? When does it occur? What is its extent?
<--- Score

103. What scope do you want your strategy to cover?
<--- Score

104. What is in the scope and what is not in scope?
<--- Score

105. Is there a completed SIPOC representation, describing the Suppliers, Inputs, Process, Outputs, and Customers?
<--- Score

106. Has the Social Data work been fairly and/or equitably divided and delegated among team members who are qualified and capable to perform the work? Has everyone contributed?
<--- Score

107. Are accountability and ownership for Social Data clearly defined?
<--- Score

108. What is the scope of the Social Data effort?
<--- Score

109. How was the 'as is' process map developed, reviewed, verified and validated?
<--- Score

110. What sources do you use to gather information for a Social Data study?
<--- Score

111. What is out-of-scope initially?
<--- Score

112. Is there a clear Social Data case definition?
<--- Score

113. How do you manage scope?
<--- Score

114. How does the Social Data manager ensure against scope creep?
<--- Score

115. Are the Social Data requirements complete?
<--- Score

116. How will variation in the actual durations of each activity be dealt with to ensure that the expected Social Data results are met?
<--- Score

117. What are the Roles and Responsibilities for each team member and its leadership? Where is this documented?
<--- Score

118. Who are the Social Data improvement team members, including Management Leads and Coaches?
<--- Score

119. Have specific policy objectives been defined?
<--- Score

120. What knowledge or experience is required?

<--- Score

121. Has the direction changed at all during the course of Social Data? If so, when did it change and why?
<--- Score

122. Will a Social Data production readiness review be required?
<--- Score

123. Is data collected and displayed to better understand customer(s) critical needs and requirements.
<--- Score

124. Is the team formed and are team leaders (Coaches and Management Leads) assigned?
<--- Score

125. How will the Social Data team and the group measure complete success of Social Data?
<--- Score

126. Is the scope of Social Data defined?
<--- Score

127. What sort of initial information to gather?
<--- Score

128. Is there a Social Data management charter, including stakeholder case, problem and goal statements, scope, milestones, roles and responsibilities, communication plan?
<--- Score

129. What baselines are required to be defined and managed?
<--- Score

130. What is a worst-case scenario for losses?
<--- Score

131. Are customer(s) identified and segmented according to their different needs and requirements?
<--- Score

132. What is in scope?
<--- Score

133. Is it clearly defined in and to your organization what you do?
<--- Score

134. When are meeting minutes sent out? Who is on the distribution list?
<--- Score

135. Who is gathering information?
<--- Score

136. Where can you gather more information?
<--- Score

137. How do you keep key subject matter experts in the loop?
<--- Score

138. Will team members regularly document their Social Data work?
<--- Score

Add up total points for this section:
_____ = Total points for this section

Divided by: _____ (number of
statements answered) = _____
Average score for this section

Transfer your score to the Social Data
Index at the beginning of the Self-
Assessment.

CRITERION #3: MEASURE:

INTENT: Gather the correct data.
Measure the current performance and
evolution of the situation.

In my belief, the answer to this
question is clearly defined:

5 Strongly Agree

4 Agree

3 Neutral

2 Disagree

1 Strongly Disagree

1. What does your operating model cost?
<--- Score

2. When should you bother with diagrams?
<--- Score

3. Do you aggressively reward and promote the
people who have the biggest impact on creating
excellent Social Data services/products?

<--- Score

4. How long to keep data and how to manage retention costs?
<--- Score

5. What are the Social Data investment costs?
<--- Score

6. Did you tackle the cause or the symptom?
<--- Score

7. What tests verify requirements?
<--- Score

8. How can you reduce costs?
<--- Score

9. Does the Social Data task fit the client's priorities?
<--- Score

10. What does a Test Case verify?
<--- Score

11. How to cause the change?
<--- Score

12. How do you measure success?
<--- Score

13. What users will be impacted?
<--- Score

14. What are the costs of reform?
<--- Score

15. How frequently do you track Social Data measures?
<--- Score

16. Is there an opportunity to verify requirements?
<--- Score

17. Are the units of measure consistent?
<--- Score

18. How will you measure your Social Data effectiveness?
<--- Score

19. Are indirect costs charged to the Social Data program?
<--- Score

20. Among the Social Data product and service cost to be estimated, which is considered hardest to estimate?
<--- Score

21. What disadvantage does this cause for the user?
<--- Score

22. How will you measure success?
<--- Score

23. Which Social Data impacts are significant?
<--- Score

24. What is an unallowable cost?
<--- Score

25. What are the uncertainties surrounding estimates

of impact?
<--- Score

26. What are the strategic priorities for this year?
<--- Score

27. At what cost?
<--- Score

28. How is the value delivered by Social Data being measured?
<--- Score

29. How will success or failure be measured?
<--- Score

30. What are the current costs of the Social Data process?
<--- Score

31. What measurements are being captured?
<--- Score

32. How is performance measured?
<--- Score

33. Are you aware of what could cause a problem?
<--- Score

34. Do you have any cost Social Data limitation requirements?
<--- Score

35. Will Social Data have an impact on current business continuity, disaster recovery processes and/ or infrastructure?

<--- Score

36. Are actual costs in line with budgeted costs?
<--- Score

37. Are missed Social Data opportunities costing your organization money?
<--- Score

38. How do you aggregate measures across priorities?
<--- Score

39. Do you effectively measure and reward individual and team performance?
<--- Score

40. What is the Social Data business impact?
<--- Score

41. What are the operational costs after Social Data deployment?
<--- Score

42. Are there any easy-to-implement alternatives to Social Data? Sometimes other solutions are available that do not require the cost implications of a full-blown project?
<--- Score

43. What is the root cause(s) of the problem?
<--- Score

44. Is the cost worth the Social Data effort ?
<--- Score

45. What are your operating costs?

<--- Score

46. How do you verify if Social Data is built right?
<--- Score

47. Is the solution cost-effective?
<--- Score

48. What do people want to verify?
<--- Score

49. How are measurements made?
<--- Score

50. Where is the cost?
<--- Score

51. What methods are feasible and acceptable to estimate the impact of reforms?
<--- Score

52. What relevant entities could be measured?
<--- Score

53. When are costs are incurred?
<--- Score

54. What could cause you to change course?
<--- Score

55. What are the costs?
<--- Score

56. Was a business case (cost/benefit) developed?
<--- Score

57. What would it cost to replace your technology?
<--- Score

58. What potential environmental factors impact the Social Data effort?
<--- Score

59. Why do the measurements/indicators matter?
<--- Score

60. Are Social Data vulnerabilities categorized and prioritized?
<--- Score

61. Which costs should be taken into account?
<--- Score

62. What is the cost of rework?
<--- Score

63. What causes extra work or rework?
<--- Score

64. What measurements are possible, practicable and meaningful?
<--- Score

65. Do you have a flow diagram of what happens?
<--- Score

66. Are there measurements based on task performance?
<--- Score

67. How can you manage cost down?
<--- Score

68. What is the cause of any Social Data gaps?
<--- Score

69. How can you measure Social Data in a systematic way?
<--- Score

70. Why do you expend time and effort to implement measurement, for whom?
<--- Score

71. Who pays the cost?
<--- Score

72. How will effects be measured?
<--- Score

73. What are the estimated costs of proposed changes?
<--- Score

74. Do you have an issue in getting priority?
<--- Score

75. What drives O&M cost?
<--- Score

76. What are the types and number of measures to use?
<--- Score

77. What are hidden Social Data quality costs?
<--- Score

78. Are the measurements objective?

<--- Score

79. How will costs be allocated?
<--- Score

80. How do you verify and develop ideas and innovations?
<--- Score

81. Are there competing Social Data priorities?
<--- Score

82. What causes mismanagement?
<--- Score

83. Is it possible to estimate the impact of unanticipated complexity such as wrong or failed assumptions, feedback, etcetera on proposed reforms?
<--- Score

84. Has a cost center been established?
<--- Score

85. How will your organization measure success?
<--- Score

86. How do you verify the Social Data requirements quality?
<--- Score

87. What evidence is there and what is measured?
<--- Score

88. When a disaster occurs, who gets priority?
<--- Score

89. What are your key Social Data organizational performance measures, including key short and longer-term financial measures?
<--- Score

90. What do you measure and why?
<--- Score

91. What can be used to verify compliance?
<--- Score

92. Have you included everything in your Social Data cost models?
<--- Score

93. Have you made assumptions about the shape of the future, particularly its impact on your customers and competitors?
<--- Score

94. Are you taking your company in the direction of better and revenue or cheaper and cost?
<--- Score

95. How will measures be used to manage and adapt?
<--- Score

96. How much does it cost?
<--- Score

97. What is your decision requirements diagram?
<--- Score

98. What are the costs and benefits?
<--- Score

99. How do you quantify and quality impacts?
<--- Score

100. Does a Social Data quantification method exist?
<--- Score

101. How is progress measured?
<--- Score

102. What does losing customers cost your organization?
<--- Score

103. What are your primary costs, revenues, assets?
<--- Score

104. What harm might be caused?
<--- Score

105. How can a Social Data test verify your ideas or assumptions?
<--- Score

106. What causes investor action?
<--- Score

107. Where is it measured?
<--- Score

108. How can you reduce the costs of obtaining inputs?
<--- Score

109. How do you verify the authenticity of the data and information used?

<--- Score

110. How do you verify your resources?
<--- Score

111. What causes innovation to fail or succeed in your organization?
<--- Score

112. What is your Social Data quality cost segregation study?
<--- Score

113. Are the Social Data benefits worth its costs?
<--- Score

114. Are supply costs steady or fluctuating?
<--- Score

115. What are allowable costs?
<--- Score

116. How do you control the overall costs of your work processes?
<--- Score

117. How do you measure variability?
<--- Score

118. Which measures and indicators matter?
<--- Score

119. Does management have the right priorities among projects?
<--- Score

120. Who should receive measurement reports?
<--- Score

121. How do you measure lifecycle phases?
<--- Score

122. What would be a real cause for concern?
<--- Score

123. What are the costs of delaying Social Data action?
<--- Score

124. What is measured? Why?
<--- Score

125. Do the benefits outweigh the costs?
<--- Score

126. How do you prevent mis-estimating cost?
<--- Score

127. How sensitive must the Social Data strategy be to cost?
<--- Score

128. What happens if cost savings do not materialize?
<--- Score

129. What are the Social Data key cost drivers?
<--- Score

130. What is the total cost related to deploying Social Data, including any consulting or professional services?
<--- Score

131. Are you able to realize any cost savings?
<--- Score

Add up total points for this section:
_____ = Total points for this section

Divided by: _____ (number of
statements answered) = _____
Average score for this section

Transfer your score to the Social Data
Index at the beginning of the Self-
Assessment.

CRITERION #4: ANALYZE:

INTENT: Analyze causes, assumptions and hypotheses.

In my belief, the answer to this question is clearly defined:

5 Strongly Agree

4 Agree

3 Neutral

2 Disagree

1 Strongly Disagree

1. How will corresponding data be collected?
<--- Score

2. What qualifications and skills do you need?
<--- Score

3. What qualifications are needed?
<--- Score

4. When should a process be art not science?

<--- Score

5. What methods do you use to gather Social Data data?
<--- Score

6. How will the Social Data data be captured?
<--- Score

7. What tools were used to narrow the list of possible causes?
<--- Score

8. What are your outputs?
<--- Score

9. How much data can be collected in the given timeframe?
<--- Score

10. Think about the functions involved in your Social Data project, what processes flow from these functions?
<--- Score

11. What were the financial benefits resulting from any 'ground fruit or low-hanging fruit' (quick fixes)?
<--- Score

12. What Social Data data should be managed?
<--- Score

13. Were Pareto charts (or similar) used to portray the 'heavy hitters' (or key sources of variation)?
<--- Score

14. What are the necessary qualifications?
<--- Score

15. Are your outputs consistent?
<--- Score

16. What Social Data data should be collected?
<--- Score

17. Is the suppliers process defined and controlled?
<--- Score

18. Is data and process analysis, root cause analysis and quantifying the gap/opportunity in place?
<--- Score

19. How do you measure the operational performance of your key work systems and processes, including productivity, cycle time, and other appropriate measures of process effectiveness, efficiency, and innovation?
<--- Score

20. What process should you select for improvement?
<--- Score

21. What are your key performance measures or indicators and in-process measures for the control and improvement of your Social Data processes?
<--- Score

22. What are the disruptive Social Data technologies that enable your organization to radically change your business processes?
<--- Score

23. How does the organization define, manage, and improve its Social Data processes?
<--- Score

24. What is your organizations process which leads to recognition of value generation?
<--- Score

25. How often will data be collected for measures?
<--- Score

26. What are the processes for audit reporting and management?
<--- Score

27. How can risk management be tied procedurally to process elements?
<--- Score

28. Who qualifies to gain access to data?
<--- Score

29. What Social Data metrics are outputs of the process?
<--- Score

30. What systems/processes must you excel at?
<--- Score

31. What resources go in to get the desired output?
<--- Score

32. What are evaluation criteria for the output?
<--- Score

33. What will drive Social Data change?

<--- Score

34. What are the revised rough estimates of the financial savings/opportunity for Social Data improvements?
<--- Score

35. What controls do you have in place to protect data?
<--- Score

36. Do staff qualifications match your project?
<--- Score

37. Who owns what data?
<--- Score

38. What are the Social Data business drivers?
<--- Score

39. What are the Social Data design outputs?
<--- Score

40. Is there any way to speed up the process?
<--- Score

41. What training and qualifications will you need?
<--- Score

42. How is Social Data data gathered?
<--- Score

43. Do your employees have the opportunity to do what they do best everyday?
<--- Score

44. What Social Data data will be collected?
<--- Score

45. What information qualified as important?
<--- Score

46. Is the required Social Data data gathered?
<--- Score

47. What do you need to qualify?
<--- Score

48. What is the Value Stream Mapping?
<--- Score

49. What were the crucial 'moments of truth' on the process map?
<--- Score

50. Who will gather what data?
<--- Score

51. Should you invest in industry-recognized qualifications?
<--- Score

52. How difficult is it to qualify what Social Data ROI is?
<--- Score

53. Are Social Data changes recognized early enough to be approved through the regular process?
<--- Score

54. Is pre-qualification of suppliers carried out?
<--- Score

55. Who gets your output?

<--- Score

56. Do quality systems drive continuous improvement?

<--- Score

57. What other organizational variables, such as reward systems or communication systems, affect the performance of this Social Data process?

<--- Score

58. What data do you need to collect?

<--- Score

59. What are the personnel training and qualifications required?

<--- Score

60. Do your contracts/agreements contain data security obligations?

<--- Score

61. What conclusions were drawn from the team's data collection and analysis? How did the team reach these conclusions?

<--- Score

62. What internal processes need improvement?

<--- Score

63. Are all team members qualified for all tasks?

<--- Score

64. What is the oversight process?

<--- Score

65. Where can you get qualified talent today?
<--- Score

66. Who is involved in the management review process?
<--- Score

67. What are your best practices for minimizing Social Data project risk, while demonstrating incremental value and quick wins throughout the Social Data project lifecycle?
<--- Score

68. What is your organizations system for selecting qualified vendors?
<--- Score

69. How do you ensure that the Social Data opportunity is realistic?
<--- Score

70. Has data output been validated?
<--- Score

71. Identify an operational issue in your organization, for example, could a particular task be done more quickly or more efficiently by Social Data?
<--- Score

72. How is the Social Data Value Stream Mapping managed?
<--- Score

73. What qualifications are necessary?

<--- Score

74. How do you promote understanding that opportunity for improvement is not criticism of the status quo, or the people who created the status quo?
<--- Score

75. Have you defined which data is gathered how?
<--- Score

76. Do your leaders quickly bounce back from setbacks?
<--- Score

77. What qualifications do Social Data leaders need?
<--- Score

78. What types of data do your Social Data indicators require?
<--- Score

79. What, related to, Social Data processes does your organization outsource?
<--- Score

80. Who is involved with workflow mapping?
<--- Score

81. Can you add value to the current Social Data decision-making process (largely qualitative) by incorporating uncertainty modeling (more quantitative)?
<--- Score

82. How is the data gathered?
<--- Score

83. What other jobs or tasks affect the performance of the steps in the Social Data process?
<--- Score

84. How do you define collaboration and team output?
<--- Score

85. A compounding model resolution with available relevant data can often provide insight towards a solution methodology; which Social Data models, tools and techniques are necessary?
<--- Score

86. Was a detailed process map created to amplify critical steps of the 'as is' stakeholder process?
<--- Score

87. Is the performance gap determined?
<--- Score

88. How has the Social Data data been gathered?
<--- Score

89. Do you understand your management processes today?
<--- Score

90. How do you use Social Data data and information to support organizational decision making and innovation?
<--- Score

91. What are your current levels and trends in key Social Data measures or indicators of product and

process performance that are important to and directly serve your customers?
<--- Score

92. What tools were used to generate the list of possible causes?
<--- Score

93. Were any designed experiments used to generate additional insight into the data analysis?
<--- Score

94. What data is gathered?
<--- Score

95. How is data used for program management and improvement?
<--- Score

96. What is the Social Data Driver?
<--- Score

97. What is the output?
<--- Score

98. Where is the data coming from to measure compliance?
<--- Score

99. Information sharing across the enterprise and integrating social data into operational processes. How close is your organization to that ideal?
<--- Score

100. How do mission and objectives affect the Social Data processes of your organization?

<--- Score

101. What are your current levels and trends in key measures or indicators of Social Data product and process performance that are important to and directly serve your customers? How do these results compare with the performance of your competitors and other organizations with similar offerings?
<--- Score

102. Are you missing Social Data opportunities?
<--- Score

103. Were there any improvement opportunities identified from the process analysis?
<--- Score

104. Do several people in different organizational units assist with the Social Data process?
<--- Score

105. What is the cost of poor quality as supported by the team's analysis?
<--- Score

106. How will the change process be managed?
<--- Score

107. Record-keeping requirements flow from the records needed as inputs, outputs, controls and for transformation of a Social Data process, are the records needed as inputs to the Social Data process available?
<--- Score

108. Do you have the authority to produce the

output?

<--- Score

109. Is the Social Data process severely broken such that a re-design is necessary?

<--- Score

110. What process improvements will be needed?

<--- Score

111. An organizationally feasible system request is one that considers the mission, goals and objectives of the organization, key questions are: is the Social Data solution request practical and will it solve a problem or take advantage of an opportunity to achieve company goals?

<--- Score

112. How do you implement and manage your work processes to ensure that they meet design requirements?

<--- Score

113. What does the data say about the performance of the stakeholder process?

<--- Score

114. What kind of crime could a potential new hire have committed that would not only not disqualify him/her from being hired by your organization, but would actually indicate that he/she might be a particularly good fit?

<--- Score

115. Is there an established change management process?

<--- Score

116. How is the way you as the leader think and process information affecting your organizational culture?
<--- Score

117. Was a cause-and-effect diagram used to explore the different types of causes (or sources of variation)?
<--- Score

118. Think about some of the processes you undertake within your organization, which do you own?
<--- Score

119. How are outputs preserved and protected?
<--- Score

120. Who will facilitate the team and process?
<--- Score

121. Has an output goal been set?
<--- Score

122. Are all staff in core Social Data subjects Highly Qualified?
<--- Score

123. How many input/output points does it require?
<--- Score

124. What is the complexity of the output produced?
<--- Score

125. What quality tools were used to get through the

analyze phase?
<--- Score

126. Is the gap/opportunity displayed and communicated in financial terms?
<--- Score

127. How do your work systems and key work processes relate to and capitalize on your core competencies?
<--- Score

128. Is there a strict change management process?
<--- Score

129. What qualifies as competition?
<--- Score

130. What did the team gain from developing a sub-process map?
<--- Score

131. Do you, as a leader, bounce back quickly from setbacks?
<--- Score

132. How will the data be checked for quality?
<--- Score

Add up total points for this section:
_ _ _ _ _ = Total points for this section

Divided by: _ _ _ _ _ _ (number of statements answered) = _ _ _ _ _ _ Average score for this section

Transfer your score to the Social Data
Index at the beginning of the Self-
Assessment.

CRITERION #5: IMPROVE:

INTENT: Develop a practical solution. Innovate, establish and test the solution and to measure the results.

In my belief, the answer to this question is clearly defined:

5 Strongly Agree

4 Agree

3 Neutral

2 Disagree

1 Strongly Disagree

1. How can you improve Social Data?
<--- Score

2. Do vendor agreements bring new compliance risk ?
<--- Score

3. What actually has to improve and by how much?
<--- Score

4. Can you identify any significant risks or exposures to Social Data third- parties (vendors, service providers, alliance partners etc) that concern you?
<--- Score

5. Is any Social Data documentation required?
<--- Score

6. How do you keep improving Social Data?
<--- Score

7. What are the affordable Social Data risks?
<--- Score

8. Who controls key decisions that will be made?
<--- Score

9. How does your organization evaluate strategic Social Data success?
<--- Score

10. Who will be responsible for making the decisions to include or exclude requested changes once Social Data is underway?
<--- Score

11. What tools do you use once you have decided on a Social Data strategy and more importantly how do you choose?
<--- Score

12. What error proofing will be done to address some of the discrepancies observed in the 'as is' process?
<--- Score

13. Is the Social Data solution sustainable?

<--- Score

14. Will the controls trigger any other risks?
<--- Score

15. What strategies for Social Data improvement are successful?
<--- Score

16. What went well, what should change, what can improve?
<--- Score

17. How can the phases of Social Data development be identified?
<--- Score

18. How do you deal with Social Data risk?
<--- Score

19. Social Data risk decisions: whose call Is It?
<--- Score

20. Do those selected for the Social Data team have a good general understanding of what Social Data is all about?
<--- Score

21. What area needs the greatest improvement?
<--- Score

22. What criteria will you use to assess your Social Data risks?
<--- Score

23. How is knowledge sharing about risk

management improved?
<--- Score

24. How do you decide how much to remunerate an employee?
<--- Score

25. What are the implications of the one critical Social Data decision 10 minutes, 10 months, and 10 years from now?
<--- Score

26. Is the Social Data risk managed?
<--- Score

27. Who are the Social Data decision-makers?
<--- Score

28. Are procedures documented for managing Social Data risks?
<--- Score

29. How can you improve performance?
<--- Score

30. Who do you report Social Data results to?
<--- Score

31. What are the Social Data security risks?
<--- Score

32. Is the solution technically practical?
<--- Score

33. How do you mitigate Social Data risk?
<--- Score

34. Explorations of the frontiers of Social Data will help you build influence, improve Social Data, optimize decision making, and sustain change, what is your approach?
<--- Score

35. How scalable is your Social Data solution?
<--- Score

36. What are the expected Social Data results?
<--- Score

37. If you could go back in time five years, what decision would you make differently? What is your best guess as to what decision you're making today you might regret five years from now?
<--- Score

38. How do you manage and improve your Social Data work systems to deliver customer value and achieve organizational success and sustainability?
<--- Score

39. Who controls the risk?
<--- Score

40. Can you integrate quality management and risk management?
<--- Score

41. Which Social Data solution is appropriate?
<--- Score

42. What current systems have to be understood and/ or changed?

<--- Score

43. What assumptions are made about the solution and approach?
<--- Score

44. Are you assessing Social Data and risk?
<--- Score

45. What to do with the results or outcomes of measurements?
<--- Score

46. Risk factors: what are the characteristics of Social Data that make it risky?
<--- Score

47. What should a proof of concept or pilot accomplish?
<--- Score

48. Do you have the optimal project management team structure?
<--- Score

49. What tools were most useful during the improve phase?
<--- Score

50. Where do you need Social Data improvement?
<--- Score

51. Are the most efficient solutions problem-specific?
<--- Score

52. Are decisions made in a timely manner?

<--- Score

53. Who should make the Social Data decisions?
<--- Score

54. Who will be using the results of the measurement activities?
<--- Score

55. How do you measure progress and evaluate training effectiveness?
<--- Score

56. How will you measure the results?
<--- Score

57. How are Social Data risks managed?
<--- Score

58. Are risk management tasks balanced centrally and locally?
<--- Score

59. Is there a high likelihood that any recommendations will achieve their intended results?
<--- Score

60. Who manages Social Data risk?
<--- Score

61. How are policy decisions made and where?
<--- Score

62. How do you improve Social Data service perception, and satisfaction?
<--- Score

63. Who makes the Social Data decisions in your organization?
<--- Score

64. Are the key business and technology risks being managed?
<--- Score

65. Risk Identification: What are the possible risk events your organization faces in relation to Social Data?
<--- Score

66. What is the team's contingency plan for potential problems occurring in implementation?
<--- Score

67. For estimation problems, how do you develop an estimation statement?
<--- Score

68. What were the underlying assumptions on the cost-benefit analysis?
<--- Score

69. What tools were used to evaluate the potential solutions?
<--- Score

70. Are the risks fully understood, reasonable and manageable?
<--- Score

71. What can you do to improve?
<--- Score

72. Who are the people involved in developing and implementing Social Data?
<--- Score

73. What is the Social Data's sustainability risk?
<--- Score

74. Which of the recognised risks out of all risks can be most likely transferred?
<--- Score

75. How do you go about comparing Social Data approaches/solutions?
<--- Score

76. Is there any other Social Data solution?
<--- Score

77. To what extent does management recognize Social Data as a tool to increase the results?
<--- Score

78. How does the team improve its work?
<--- Score

79. What practices helps your organization to develop its capacity to recognize patterns?
<--- Score

80. Who are the key stakeholders for the Social Data evaluation?
<--- Score

81. What is the magnitude of the improvements?
<--- Score

82. Is the Social Data documentation thorough?
<--- Score

83. Would you develop a Social Data Communication Strategy?
<--- Score

84. What alternative responses are available to manage risk?
<--- Score

85. What is Social Data's impact on utilizing the best solution(s)?
<--- Score

86. What lessons, if any, from a pilot were incorporated into the design of the full-scale solution?
<--- Score

87. Are risk triggers captured?
<--- Score

88. Is the scope clearly documented?
<--- Score

89. How risky is your organization?
<--- Score

90. When you map the key players in your own work and the types/domains of relationships with them, which relationships do you find easy and which challenging, and why?
<--- Score

91. How do you measure risk?

<--- Score

92. For decision problems, how do you develop a decision statement?
<--- Score

93. What risks do you need to manage?
<--- Score

94. Are events managed to resolution?
<--- Score

95. How do you link measurement and risk?
<--- Score

96. Have you achieved Social Data improvements?
<--- Score

97. In the past few months, what is the smallest change you have made that has had the biggest positive result? What was it about that small change that produced the large return?
<--- Score

98. Does a good decision guarantee a good outcome?
<--- Score

99. Who manages supplier risk management in your organization?
<--- Score

100. Is Social Data documentation maintained?
<--- Score

101. Is the measure of success for Social Data understandable to a variety of people?

<--- Score

102. How do you manage Social Data risk?
<--- Score

103. What is the risk?
<--- Score

104. Why improve in the first place?
<--- Score

105. How do you improve productivity?
<--- Score

106. How will you know that a change is an improvement?
<--- Score

107. How can you better manage risk?
<--- Score

108. What improvements have been achieved?
<--- Score

109. Can the solution be designed and implemented within an acceptable time period?
<--- Score

110. Who are the Social Data decision makers?
<--- Score

111. What do you want to improve?
<--- Score

112. How will you know when its improved?
<--- Score

113. How will you recognize and celebrate results?
<--- Score

114. What needs improvement? Why?
<--- Score

115. Does the goal represent a desired result that can be measured?
<--- Score

116. How will you know that you have improved?
<--- Score

117. What is the implementation plan?
<--- Score

118. Do you cover the five essential competencies: Communication, Collaboration,Innovation, Adaptability, and Leadership that improve an organizations ability to leverage the new Social Data in a volatile global economy?
<--- Score

119. Is risk periodically assessed?
<--- Score

120. What tools were used to tap into the creativity and encourage 'outside the box' thinking?
<--- Score

121. What are your current levels and trends in key measures or indicators of workforce and leader development?
<--- Score

122. How do you improve your likelihood of success ?
<--- Score

123. How can skill-level changes improve Social Data?
<--- Score

124. Where do the Social Data decisions reside?
<--- Score

125. What are the concrete Social Data results?
<--- Score

126. Was a Social Data charter developed?
<--- Score

127. What is Social Data risk?
<--- Score

128. How is continuous improvement applied to risk management?
<--- Score

129. Have you identified breakpoints and/or risk tolerances that will trigger broad consideration of a potential need for intervention or modification of strategy?
<--- Score

130. Risk events: what are the things that could go wrong?
<--- Score

Add up total points for this section:
_ _ _ _ _ = Total points for this section

Divided by: _ _ _ _ _ _ (number of

statements answered) = _____
Average score for this section

Transfer your score to the Social Data
Index at the beginning of the Self-
Assessment.

CRITERION #6: CONTROL:

INTENT: Implement the practical solution. Maintain the performance and correct possible complications.

In my belief, the answer to this question is clearly defined:

5 Strongly Agree

4 Agree

3 Neutral

2 Disagree

1 Strongly Disagree

1. How will the day-to-day responsibilities for monitoring and continual improvement be transferred from the improvement team to the process owner?
<--- Score

2. What is your plan to assess your security risks?
<--- Score

3. Is there an action plan in case of emergencies?
<--- Score

4. Are documented procedures clear and easy to follow for the operators?
<--- Score

5. Are suggested corrective/restorative actions indicated on the response plan for known causes to problems that might surface?
<--- Score

6. Will the team be available to assist members in planning investigations?
<--- Score

7. What are the critical parameters to watch?
<--- Score

8. How do you plan on providing proper recognition and disclosure of supporting companies?
<--- Score

9. What are the key elements of your Social Data performance improvement system, including your evaluation, organizational learning, and innovation processes?
<--- Score

10. Will any special training be provided for results interpretation?
<--- Score

11. How will report readings be checked to effectively monitor performance?
<--- Score

12. Is there a control plan in place for sustaining improvements (short and long-term)?
<--- Score

13. Who will be in control?
<--- Score

14. Have new or revised work instructions resulted?
<--- Score

15. Against what alternative is success being measured?
<--- Score

16. Can you adapt and adjust to changing Social Data situations?
<--- Score

17. How do you select, collect, align, and integrate Social Data data and information for tracking daily operations and overall organizational performance, including progress relative to strategic objectives and action plans?
<--- Score

18. Is there a Social Data Communication plan covering who needs to get what information when?
<--- Score

19. Will your goals reflect your program budget?
<--- Score

20. Does the Social Data performance meet the customer's requirements?
<--- Score

21. Are you measuring, monitoring and predicting Social Data activities to optimize operations and profitability, and enhancing outcomes?
<--- Score

22. How can you best use all of your knowledge repositories to enhance learning and sharing?
<--- Score

23. Who is going to spread your message?
<--- Score

24. How do you spread information?
<--- Score

25. Are there documented procedures?
<--- Score

26. Does Social Data appropriately measure and monitor risk?
<--- Score

27. Act/Adjust: What Do you Need to Do Differently?
<--- Score

28. How widespread is its use?
<--- Score

29. Do the Social Data decisions you make today help people and the planet tomorrow?
<--- Score

30. You may have created your quality measures at a time when you lacked resources, technology wasn't up to the required standard, or low service levels

were the industry norm. Have those circumstances changed?
<--- Score

31. Who controls critical resources?
<--- Score

32. How do senior leaders actions reflect a commitment to the organizations Social Data values?
<--- Score

33. What is the best design framework for Social Data organization now that, in a post industrial-age if the top-down, command and control model is no longer relevant?
<--- Score

34. What is the recommended frequency of auditing?
<--- Score

35. Who sets the Social Data standards?
<--- Score

36. In the case of a Social Data project, the criteria for the audit derive from implementation objectives, an audit of a Social Data project involves assessing whether the recommendations outlined for implementation have been met, can you track that any Social Data project is implemented as planned, and is it working?
<--- Score

37. What are the performance and scale of the Social Data tools?
<--- Score

38. Are pertinent alerts monitored, analyzed and distributed to appropriate personnel?
<--- Score

39. Is a response plan established and deployed?
<--- Score

40. How do you monitor usage and cost?
<--- Score

41. Will existing staff require re-training, for example, to learn new business processes?
<--- Score

42. Do the viable solutions scale to future needs?
<--- Score

43. Is there a standardized process?
<--- Score

44. How do you establish and deploy modified action plans if circumstances require a shift in plans and rapid execution of new plans?
<--- Score

45. Are the Social Data standards challenging?
<--- Score

46. How do you encourage people to take control and responsibility?
<--- Score

47. Who has control over resources?
<--- Score

48. How will the process owner verify improvement in

present and future sigma levels, process capabilities?
<--- Score

49. Do you monitor the Social Data decisions made and fine tune them as they evolve?
<--- Score

50. Is a response plan in place for when the input, process, or output measures indicate an 'out-of-control' condition?
<--- Score

51. Are operating procedures consistent?
<--- Score

52. Is there documentation that will support the successful operation of the improvement?
<--- Score

53. What is the control/monitoring plan?
<--- Score

54. Are the planned controls working?
<--- Score

55. Has the Social Data value of standards been quantified?
<--- Score

56. Do you monitor the effectiveness of your Social Data activities?
<--- Score

57. Does a troubleshooting guide exist or is it needed?
<--- Score

58. Can support from partners be adjusted?
<--- Score

59. Is there a documented and implemented monitoring plan?
<--- Score

60. How do you plan for the cost of succession?
<--- Score

61. What other areas of the group might benefit from the Social Data team's improvements, knowledge, and learning?
<--- Score

62. How do controls support value?
<--- Score

63. Are the planned controls in place?
<--- Score

64. Are new process steps, standards, and documentation ingrained into normal operations?
<--- Score

65. How will new or emerging customer needs/requirements be checked/communicated to orient the process toward meeting the new specifications and continually reducing variation?
<--- Score

66. How might the group capture best practices and lessons learned so as to leverage improvements?
<--- Score

67. How is Social Data project cost planned, managed,

monitored?
<--- Score

68. What are customers monitoring?
<--- Score

69. What other systems, operations, processes, and infrastructures (hiring practices, staffing, training, incentives/rewards, metrics/dashboards/scorecards, etc.) need updates, additions, changes, or deletions in order to facilitate knowledge transfer and improvements?
<--- Score

70. Who is the Social Data process owner?
<--- Score

71. What should you measure to verify efficiency gains?
<--- Score

72. Is knowledge gained on process shared and institutionalized?
<--- Score

73. How will the process owner and team be able to hold the gains?
<--- Score

74. What are you attempting to measure/monitor?
<--- Score

75. How is change control managed?
<--- Score

76. What is the standard for acceptable Social Data

performance?
<--- Score

77. What is your theory of human motivation, and how does your compensation plan fit with that view?
<--- Score

78. Is new knowledge gained imbedded in the response plan?
<--- Score

79. Has the improved process and its steps been standardized?
<--- Score

80. Is reporting being used or needed?
<--- Score

81. What are your results for key measures or indicators of the accomplishment of your Social Data strategy and action plans, including building and strengthening core competencies?
<--- Score

82. How will Social Data decisions be made and monitored?
<--- Score

83. Does the response plan contain a definite closed loop continual improvement scheme (e.g., plan-do-check-act)?
<--- Score

84. How will input, process, and output variables be checked to detect for sub-optimal conditions?
<--- Score

85. How likely is the current Social Data plan to come in on schedule or on budget?
<--- Score

86. Is there a recommended audit plan for routine surveillance inspections of Social Data's gains?
<--- Score

87. What adjustments to the strategies are needed?
<--- Score

88. Is there a transfer of ownership and knowledge to process owner and process team tasked with the responsibilities.
<--- Score

89. What do your reports reflect?
<--- Score

90. Does job training on the documented procedures need to be part of the process team's education and training?
<--- Score

91. What can you control?
<--- Score

92. What quality tools were useful in the control phase?
<--- Score

93. Are controls in place and consistently applied?
<--- Score

94. How will you measure your QA plan's

effectiveness?
<--- Score

95. What key inputs and outputs are being measured on an ongoing basis?
<--- Score

96. How do your controls stack up?
<--- Score

97. Where do ideas that reach policy makers and planners as proposals for Social Data strengthening and reform actually originate?
<--- Score

98. Implementation Planning: is a pilot needed to test the changes before a full roll out occurs?
<--- Score

99. What should the next improvement project be that is related to Social Data?
<--- Score

Add up total points for this section:
_ _ _ _ _ = Total points for this section

Divided by: _ _ _ _ _ _ (number of statements answered) = _ _ _ _ _ _
Average score for this section

Transfer your score to the Social Data Index at the beginning of the Self-Assessment.

CRITERION #7: SUSTAIN:

INTENT: Retain the benefits.

In my belief, the answer to this question is clearly defined:

5 Strongly Agree

4 Agree

3 Neutral

2 Disagree

1 Strongly Disagree

1. Are your responses positive or negative?
<--- Score

2. Is your strategy driving your strategy? Or is the way in which you allocate resources driving your strategy?
<--- Score

3. Who is responsible for Social Data?
<--- Score

4. Whom among your colleagues do you trust, and for

what?
<--- Score

5. How is implementation research currently incorporated into each of your goals?
<--- Score

6. Why should people listen to you?
<--- Score

7. Are you satisfied with your current role? If not, what is missing from it?
<--- Score

8. Can you maintain your growth without detracting from the factors that have contributed to your success?
<--- Score

9. If you had to leave your organization for a year and the only communication you could have with employees/colleagues was a single paragraph, what would you write?
<--- Score

10. How can you become more high-tech but still be high touch?
<--- Score

11. What happens at your organization when people fail?
<--- Score

12. What is the recommended frequency of auditing?
<--- Score

13. Are you relevant? Will you be relevant five years from now? Ten?
<--- Score

14. How do customers see your organization?
<--- Score

15. Are there any activities that you can take off your to do list?
<--- Score

16. What happens when a new employee joins the organization?
<--- Score

17. Who will manage the integration of tools?
<--- Score

18. What is your BATNA (best alternative to a negotiated agreement)?
<--- Score

19. Why will customers want to buy your organizations products/services?
<--- Score

20. How do you foster the skills, knowledge, talents, attributes, and characteristics you want to have?
<--- Score

21. What trouble can you get into?
<--- Score

22. Is there any existing Social Data governance structure?
<--- Score

23. In a project to restructure Social Data outcomes, which stakeholders would you involve?
<--- Score

24. What is the estimated value of the project?
<--- Score

25. Is a Social Data team work effort in place?
<--- Score

26. Do you know who is a friend or a foe?
<--- Score

27. How can you incorporate support to ensure safe and effective use of Social Data into the services that you provide?
<--- Score

28. Operational - will it work?
<--- Score

29. Who is responsible for errors?
<--- Score

30. What are specific Social Data rules to follow?
<--- Score

31. How do you keep records, of what?
<--- Score

32. How do you govern and fulfill your societal responsibilities?
<--- Score

33. What should you stop doing?

<--- Score

34. Are you paying enough attention to the partners your company depends on to succeed?
<--- Score

35. How do you assess the Social Data pitfalls that are inherent in implementing it?
<--- Score

36. If you find that you havent accomplished one of the goals for one of the steps of the Social Data strategy, what will you do to fix it?
<--- Score

37. How will you motivate the stakeholders with the least vested interest?
<--- Score

38. If there were zero limitations, what would you do differently?
<--- Score

39. What is the range of capabilities?
<--- Score

40. How will you insure seamless interoperability of Social Data moving forward?
<--- Score

41. Is there any reason to believe the opposite of my current belief?
<--- Score

42. What does your signature ensure?
<--- Score

43. Why should you adopt a Social Data framework?
<--- Score

44. If you got fired and a new hire took your place, what would she do different?
<--- Score

45. Who have you, as a company, historically been when you've been at your best?
<--- Score

46. Ask yourself: how would you do this work if you only had one staff member to do it?
<--- Score

47. How much does Social Data help?
<--- Score

48. What new services of functionality will be implemented next with Social Data ?
<--- Score

49. When information truly is ubiquitous, when reach and connectivity are completely global, when computing resources are infinite, and when a whole new set of impossibilities are not only possible, but happening, what will that do to your business?
<--- Score

50. What may be the consequences for the performance of an organization if all stakeholders are not consulted regarding Social Data?
<--- Score

51. How do you track customer value, profitability

or financial return, organizational success, and sustainability?
<--- Score

52. How do you listen to customers to obtain actionable information?
<--- Score

53. Is it economical; do you have the time and money?
<--- Score

54. What stupid rule would you most like to kill?
<--- Score

55. How do you set Social Data stretch targets and how do you get people to not only participate in setting these stretch targets but also that they strive to achieve these?
<--- Score

56. What are the short and long-term Social Data goals?
<--- Score

57. How do you provide a safe environment -physically and emotionally?
<--- Score

58. What are the barriers to increased Social Data production?
<--- Score

59. Who is on the team?
<--- Score

60. Did your employees make progress today?

<--- Score

61. What are current Social Data paradigms?
<--- Score

62. How do you deal with Social Data changes?
<--- Score

63. Are the assumptions believable and achievable?
<--- Score

64. Who, on the executive team or the board, has spoken to a customer recently?
<--- Score

65. Have benefits been optimized with all key stakeholders?
<--- Score

66. What would you recommend your friend do if he/she were facing this dilemma?
<--- Score

67. What are strategies for increasing support and reducing opposition?
<--- Score

68. Marketing budgets are tighter, consumers are more skeptical, and social media has changed forever the way we talk about Social Data, how do you gain traction?
<--- Score

69. Do you have past Social Data successes?
<--- Score

70. What will be the consequences to the stakeholder (financial, reputation etc) if Social Data does not go ahead or fails to deliver the objectives?
<--- Score

71. Which individuals, teams or departments will be involved in Social Data?
<--- Score

72. How are you doing compared to your industry?
<--- Score

73. Do you say no to customers for no reason?
<--- Score

74. Who are four people whose careers you have enhanced?
<--- Score

75. How do you lead with Social Data in mind?
<--- Score

76. At what moment would you think; Will I get fired?
<--- Score

77. What are you trying to prove to yourself, and how might it be hijacking your life and business success?
<--- Score

78. Are you / should you be revolutionary or evolutionary?
<--- Score

79. Who will provide the final approval of Social Data deliverables?
<--- Score

80. Is there a work around that you can use?
<--- Score

81. What are the rules and assumptions your industry operates under? What if the opposite were true?
<--- Score

82. What must you excel at?
<--- Score

83. How do you go about securing Social Data?
<--- Score

84. What are the business goals Social Data is aiming to achieve?
<--- Score

85. How do you proactively clarify deliverables and Social Data quality expectations?
<--- Score

86. How likely is it that a customer would recommend your company to a friend or colleague?
<--- Score

87. In the past year, what have you done (or could you have done) to increase the accurate perception of your company/brand as ethical and honest?
<--- Score

88. How do you make it meaningful in connecting Social Data with what users do day-to-day?
<--- Score

89. What are the key enablers to make this Social Data

move?
<--- Score

90. What is effective Social Data?
<--- Score

91. What is your formula for success in Social Data ?
<--- Score

92. Where can you break convention?
<--- Score

93. Is a Social Data breakthrough on the horizon?
<--- Score

94. If you do not follow, then how to lead?
<--- Score

95. How do you stay inspired?
<--- Score

96. Is your basic point _____ or _____?
<--- Score

97. Will it be accepted by users?
<--- Score

98. How do you engage the workforce, in addition to satisfying them?
<--- Score

99. What management system can you use to leverage the Social Data experience, ideas, and concerns of the people closest to the work to be done?
<--- Score

100. What are you challenging?
<--- Score

101. To whom do you add value?
<--- Score

102. What have you done to protect your business from competitive encroachment?
<--- Score

103. What are the challenges?
<--- Score

104. How do you create buy-in?
<--- Score

105. How does Social Data integrate with other stakeholder initiatives?
<--- Score

106. What are the potential basics of Social Data fraud?
<--- Score

107. What would have to be true for the option on the table to be the best possible choice?
<--- Score

108. Do you know what you are doing? And who do you call if you don't?
<--- Score

109. What are the essentials of internal Social Data management?
<--- Score

110. Are assumptions made in Social Data stated explicitly?
<--- Score

111. What is the overall talent health of your organization as a whole at senior levels, and for each organization reporting to a member of the Senior Leadership Team?
<--- Score

112. Who is responsible for ensuring appropriate resources (time, people and money) are allocated to Social Data?
<--- Score

113. How do you know if you are successful?
<--- Score

114. Do you think you know, or do you know you know ?
<--- Score

115. Political -is anyone trying to undermine this project?
<--- Score

116. If no one would ever find out about your accomplishments, how would you lead differently?
<--- Score

117. Why not do Social Data?
<--- Score

118. What relationships among Social Data trends do you perceive?

<--- Score

119. Do you feel that more should be done in the Social Data area?
<--- Score

120. What role does communication play in the success or failure of a Social Data project?
<--- Score

121. What are the success criteria that will indicate that Social Data objectives have been met and the benefits delivered?
<--- Score

122. What goals did you miss?
<--- Score

123. Whose voice (department, ethnic group, women, older workers, etc) might you have missed hearing from in your company, and how might you amplify this voice to create positive momentum for your business?
<--- Score

124. How do you foster innovation?
<--- Score

125. What is a feasible sequencing of reform initiatives over time?
<--- Score

126. What are internal and external Social Data relations?
<--- Score

127. Which functions and people interact with the supplier and or customer?
<--- Score

128. What could happen if you do not do it?
<--- Score

129. How much contingency will be available in the budget?
<--- Score

130. Are you making progress, and are you making progress as Social Data leaders?
<--- Score

131. What is your question? Why?
<--- Score

132. Why is Social Data important for you now?
<--- Score

133. How will you know that the Social Data project has been successful?
<--- Score

134. If you were responsible for initiating and implementing major changes in your organization, what steps might you take to ensure acceptance of those changes?
<--- Score

135. How do you keep the momentum going?
<--- Score

136. Who are your customers?
<--- Score

137. Are all key stakeholders present at all Structured Walkthroughs?
<--- Score

138. What do we do when new problems arise?
<--- Score

139. Are you using a design thinking approach and integrating Innovation, Social Data Experience, and Brand Value?
<--- Score

140. What you are going to do to affect the numbers?
<--- Score

141. Think of your Social Data project, what are the main functions?
<--- Score

142. What is the funding source for this project?
<--- Score

143. How do you ensure that implementations of Social Data products are done in a way that ensures safety?
<--- Score

144. Who will be responsible for deciding whether Social Data goes ahead or not after the initial investigations?
<--- Score

145. How do you accomplish your long range Social Data goals?
<--- Score

146. How can you negotiate Social Data successfully with a stubborn boss, an irate client, or a deceitful coworker?
<--- Score

147. What is it like to work for you?
<--- Score

148. Who do you think the world wants your organization to be?
<--- Score

149. What is the big Social Data idea?
<--- Score

150. Who will determine interim and final deadlines?
<--- Score

151. What is your Social Data strategy?
<--- Score

152. Is Social Data realistic, or are you setting yourself up for failure?
<--- Score

153. What one word do you want to own in the minds of your customers, employees, and partners?
<--- Score

154. How long will it take to change?
<--- Score

155. Are new benefits received and understood?
<--- Score

156. If your company went out of business tomorrow, would anyone who doesn't get a paycheck here care?
<--- Score

157. What business benefits will Social Data goals deliver if achieved?
<--- Score

158. What is the craziest thing you can do?
<--- Score

159. What is something you believe that nearly no one agrees with you on?
<--- Score

160. Who do we want your customers to become?
<--- Score

161. Were lessons learned captured and communicated?
<--- Score

162. What is an unauthorized commitment?
<--- Score

163. What Social Data modifications can you make work for you?
<--- Score

164. Do you have the right capabilities and capacities?
<--- Score

165. Which models, tools and techniques are necessary?
<--- Score

166. Can you break it down?
<--- Score

167. Would you rather sell to knowledgeable and informed customers or to uninformed customers?
<--- Score

168. Have new benefits been realized?
<--- Score

169. What Social Data skills are most important?
<--- Score

170. What are your most important goals for the strategic Social Data objectives?
<--- Score

171. If your customer were your grandmother, would you tell her to buy what you're selling?
<--- Score

172. How do you manage Social Data Knowledge Management (KM)?
<--- Score

173. What are the usability implications of Social Data actions?
<--- Score

174. What did you miss in the interview for the worst hire you ever made?
<--- Score

175. Will there be any necessary staff changes (redundancies or new hires)?
<--- Score

176. Do you think Social Data accomplishes the goals you expect it to accomplish?
<--- Score

177. What is the purpose of Social Data in relation to the mission?
<--- Score

178. What projects are going on in the organization today, and what resources are those projects using from the resource pools?
<--- Score

179. Can you do all this work?
<--- Score

180. How do senior leaders deploy your organizations vision and values through your leadership system, to the workforce, to key suppliers and partners, and to customers and other stakeholders, as appropriate?
<--- Score

181. Which Social Data goals are the most important?
<--- Score

182. How do you transition from the baseline to the target?
<--- Score

183. What are the gaps in your knowledge and experience?
<--- Score

184. What knowledge, skills and characteristics mark a good Social Data project manager?

<--- Score

185. Is the impact that Social Data has shown?
<--- Score

186. What are the top 3 things at the forefront of your Social Data agendas for the next 3 years?
<--- Score

187. What was the last experiment you ran?
<--- Score

188. What is the source of the strategies for Social Data strengthening and reform?
<--- Score

189. Who uses your product in ways you never expected?
<--- Score

190. Do you see more potential in people than they do in themselves?
<--- Score

191. How will you ensure you get what you expected?
<--- Score

192. What are the long-term Social Data goals?
<--- Score

193. Why do and why don't your customers like your organization?
<--- Score

194. Are you changing as fast as the world around you?

<--- Score

195. Why is it important to have senior management support for a Social Data project?
<--- Score

196. What is the overall business strategy?
<--- Score

197. What potential megatrends could make your business model obsolete?
<--- Score

198. Do you have the right people on the bus?
<--- Score

199. Do Social Data rules make a reasonable demand on a users capabilities?
<--- Score

200. How important is Social Data to the user organizations mission?
<--- Score

201. How do you determine the key elements that affect Social Data workforce satisfaction, how are these elements determined for different workforce groups and segments?
<--- Score

202. What are your personal philosophies regarding Social Data and how do they influence your work?
<--- Score

203. Has implementation been effective in reaching specified objectives so far?

<--- Score

204. If you had to rebuild your organization without any traditional competitive advantages (i.e., no killer technology, promising research, innovative product/ service delivery model, etcetera), how would your people have to approach their work and collaborate together in order to create the necessary conditions for success?
<--- Score

205. Who are the key stakeholders?
<--- Score

206. Do you have enough freaky customers in your portfolio pushing you to the limit day in and day out?
<--- Score

207. What trophy do you want on your mantle?
<--- Score

208. Who do you want your customers to become?
<--- Score

209. What happens if you do not have enough funding?
<--- Score

210. Are you maintaining a past–present–future perspective throughout the Social Data discussion?
<--- Score

211. Instead of going to current contacts for new ideas, what if you reconnected with dormant contacts--the people you used to know? If you were going reactivate a dormant tie, who would it be?

<--- Score

212. What have been your experiences in defining long range Social Data goals?
<--- Score

213. What information is critical to your organization that your executives are ignoring?
<--- Score

214. If you weren't already in this business, would you enter it today? And if not, what are you going to do about it?
<--- Score

215. How can you become the company that would put you out of business?
<--- Score

216. How do you maintain Social Data's Integrity?
<--- Score

Add up total points for this section:
_____ = Total points for this section

Divided by: _____ (number of
statements answered) = _____
Average score for this section

Transfer your score to the Social Data
Index at the beginning of the Self-
Assessment.

Social Data and Managing Projects, Criteria for Project Managers:

1.0 Initiating Process Group: Social Data

1. What do you need to do?

2. What are the constraints?

3. Specific - is the objective clear in terms of what, how, when, and where the situation will be changed?

4. How can you make your needs known?

5. Based on your Social Data project communication management plan, what worked well?

6. Just how important is your work to the overall success of the Social Data project?

7. Do you know the roles & responsibilities required for this Social Data project?

8. What is the NEXT thing to do?

9. Are identified risks being monitored properly, are new risks arising during the Social Data project or are foreseen risks occurring?

10. Professionals want to know what is expected from them what are the deliverables?

11. What were things that you did well, and could improve, and how?

12. Who is performing the work of the Social Data project?

13. Who supports, improves, and oversees standardized processes related to the Social Data projects program?

14. What are the inputs required to produce the deliverables?

15. Does it make any difference if you am successful?

16. Mitigate. what will you do to minimize the impact should the risk event occur?

17. First of all, should any action be taken?

18. When are the deliverables to be generated in each phase?

19. What will you do?

20. During which stage of Risk planning are risks prioritized based on probability and impact?

1.1 Project Charter: Social Data

21. What is in it for you?

22. Environmental stewardship and sustainability considerations: what is the process that will be used to ensure compliance with the environmental stewardship policy?

23. If finished, on what date did it finish?

24. Social Data project deliverables: what is the Social Data project going to produce?

25. What are the assumptions?

26. Fit with other Products Compliments – Cannibalizes?

27. What barriers do you predict to your success?

28. Run it as as a startup?

29. Assumptions and constraints: what assumptions were made in defining the Social Data project?

30. Who manages integration?

31. What is the justification?

32. Is it an improvement over existing products?

33. Are there special technology requirements?

34. What are some examples of a business case?

35. Who will take notes, document decisions?

36. When will this occur?

37. Is time of the essence?

38. What is the purpose of the Social Data project?

39. Why use a Social Data project charter?

40. Dependent Social Data projects: what Social Data projects must be underway or completed before this Social Data project can be successful?

1.2 Stakeholder Register: Social Data

41. How much influence do they have on the Social Data project?

42. Is your organization ready for change?

43. Who wants to talk about Security?

44. How should employers make voices heard?

45. What are the major Social Data project milestones requiring communications or providing communications opportunities?

46. What & Why?

47. How big is the gap?

48. How will reports be created?

49. Who are the stakeholders?

50. What opportunities exist to provide communications?

51. Who is managing stakeholder engagement?

52. What is the power of the stakeholder?

1.3 Stakeholder Analysis Matrix: Social Data

53. Philosophy and values?

54. Partnerships, agencies, distribution?

55. Who will be affected by the Social Data project?

56. Do any safeguard policies apply to the Social Data project?

57. Who is influential in the Social Data project area (both thematic and geographic areas)?

58. Management cover, succession?

59. What can the stakeholder prevent from happening?

60. Global influences?

61. Cashflow, start-up cash-drain?

62. What mechanisms are proposed to monitor and measure Social Data project performance in terms of social development outcomes?

63. Is there evidence that demonstrates the impact of education on the Social Data projects outcomes?

64. How do customers express needs?

65. Which conditions out of the control of the management are crucial for the sustainability of its effects?

66. Price, value, quality?

67. What do you Evaluate?

68. Sustainable financial backing?

69. Who will obstruct/hinder the Social Data project if they are not involved?

70. What are the opportunities for communication?

71. How to involve media?

72. Environmental effects?

2.0 Planning Process Group: Social Data

73. In what way has the program contributed towards the issue culture and development included on the public agenda?

74. Did the program design/ implementation strategy adequately address the planning stage necessary to set up structures, hire staff etc.?

75. Is your organization showing technical capacity and leadership commitment to keep working with the Social Data project and to repeat it?

76. What should you do next?

77. Is the identification of the problems, inequalities and gaps, with respective causes, clear in the Social Data project?

78. Did you read it correctly?

79. Contingency planning. if a risk event occurs, what will you do?

80. Just how important is your work to the overall success of the Social Data project?

81. What type of estimation method are you using?

82. If a risk event occurs, what will you do?

83. In what way has the Social Data project come up with innovative measures for problem-solving?

84. How should needs be met?

85. To what extent and in what ways are the Social Data project contributing to progress towards organizational reform?

86. Have operating capacities been created and/or reinforced in partners?

87. What is involved in Social Data project scope management, and why is good Social Data project scope management so important on information technology Social Data projects?

88. How are it Social Data projects different?

89. Does the program have follow-up mechanisms (to verify the quality of the products, punctuality of delivery, etc.) to measure progress in the achievement of the envisaged results?

90. To what extent have public/private national resources and/or counterparts been mobilized to contribute to the programs objective and produce results and impacts?

2.1 Project Management Plan: Social Data

91. What are the assigned resources?

92. Was the peer (technical) review of the cost estimates duly coordinated with the cost estimate center of expertise and addressed in the review documentation and certification?

93. Is the budget realistic?

94. What goes into your Social Data project Charter?

95. What should you drop in order to add something new?

96. What are the training needs?

97. Are there any scope changes proposed for a previously authorized Social Data project?

98. When is the Social Data project management plan created?

99. Is the appropriate plan selected based on your organizations objectives and evaluation criteria expressed in Principles and Guidelines policies?

100. What went right?

101. Did the planning effort collaborate to develop solutions that integrate expertise, policies, programs,

and Social Data projects across entities?

102. Where does all this information come from?

103. Who is the sponsor?

104. What worked well?

105. Are there any windfall benefits that would accrue to the Social Data project sponsor or other parties?

106. Are the existing and future without-plan conditions reasonable and appropriate?

107. Has the selected plan been formulated using cost effectiveness and incremental analysis techniques?

108. When is a Social Data project management plan created?

109. Is the engineering content at a feasibility level-of-detail, and is it sufficiently complete, to provide an adequate basis for the baseline cost estimate?

2.2 Scope Management Plan: Social Data

110. What problem is being solved by delivering this Social Data project?

111. Are internal Social Data project status meetings held at reasonable intervals?

112. Are Social Data project team members involved in detailed estimating and scheduling?

113. Does the title convey to the reader the essence of the Social Data project?

114. Are all payments made according to the contract(s)?

115. Has the Social Data project manager been identified?

116. What happens if scope changes?

117. Is mitigation authorized or recommended?

118. What is the need the Social Data project will address?

119. Have the procedures for identifying budget variances been followed?

120. Are Social Data project team members committed fulltime?

121. Is there a Steering Committee in place?

122. Are there procedures in place to effectively manage interdependencies with other Social Data projects, systems, Vendors and your organizations work effort?

123. During what part of the PM process is the Social Data project scope statement created?

124. What are the risks of not having good inter-organization cooperation on the Social Data project?

125. How much money have you spent?

126. Is it possible to track all classes of Social Data project work (e.g. scheduled, un-scheduled, defect repair, etc.)?

127. Have adequate procedures been put in place for Social Data project communication and status reporting across Social Data project boundaries (for example interdependent software development among interfacing systems)?

128. What went wrong?

2.3 Requirements Management Plan: Social Data

129. Have stakeholders been instructed in the Change Control process?

130. What information regarding the Social Data project requirements will be reported?

131. Are actual resources expenditures versus planned expenditures acceptable?

132. After the requirements are gathered and set forth on the requirements register, theyre little more than a laundry list of items. Some may be duplicates, some might conflict with others and some will be too broad or too vague to understand. Describe how the requirements will be analyzed. Who will perform the analysis?

133. What is the earliest finish date for this Social Data project if it is scheduled to start on ...?

134. How will requirements be managed?

135. The wbs is developed as part of a joint planning session. and how do you know that youhave done this right?

136. How will you communicate scheduled tasks to other team members?

137. Define the help desk model. who will take full

responsibility?

138. Who has the authority to reject Social Data project requirements?

139. Will the product release be stable and mature enough to be deployed In the user communIty?

140. Will you use an assessment of the Social Data project environment as a tool to discover risk to the requirements process?

141. Will the contractors involved take full responsibility?

142. What cost metrics will be used?

143. Has the requirements team been instructed in the Change Control process?

144. Why manage requirements?

145. Did you get proper approvals?

146. Are actual resource expenditures versus planned still acceptable?

147. How will you develop the schedule of requirements activities?

148. Who will approve the requirements (and if multiple approvers, in what order)?

2.4 Requirements Documentation: Social Data

149. Who is involved?

150. Is new technology needed?

151. The problem with gathering requirements is right there in the word gathering. What images does it conjure?

152. What kind of entity is a problem ?

153. Do your constraints stand?

154. What will be the integration problems?

155. What marketing channels do you want to use: e-mail, letter or sms?

156. What are the attributes of a customer?

157. How does the proposed Social Data project contribute to the overall objectives of your organization?

158. What are the potential disadvantages/ advantages?

159. Can the requirement be changed without a large impact on other requirements?

160. Basic work/business process; high-level, what is

being touched?

161. Can you check system requirements?

162. Who is interacting with the system?

163. Does your organization restrict technical alternatives?

164. What images does it conjure?

165. What is effective documentation?

166. If applicable; are there issues linked with the fact that this is an offshore Social Data project?

167. How do you get the user to tell you what they want?

2.5 Requirements Traceability Matrix: Social Data

168. How will it affect the stakeholders personally in career?

169. What is the WBS?

170. Why use a WBS?

171. How do you manage scope?

172. Why do you manage scope?

173. Describe the process for approving requirements so they can be added to the traceability matrix and Social Data project work can be performed. Will the Social Data project requirements become approved in writing?

174. What are the chronologies, contingencies, consequences, criteria?

175. Do you have a clear understanding of all subcontracts in place?

176. How small is small enough?

177. Will you use a Requirements Traceability Matrix?

178. What percentage of Social Data projects are producing traceability matrices between requirements and other work products?

179. Is there a requirements traceability process in place?

2.6 Project Scope Statement: Social Data

180. Is there a baseline plan against which to measure progress?

181. Is the change control process documented and on file?

182. Have the reports to be produced, distributed, and filed been defined?

183. Is the scope of your Social Data project well defined?

184. Will an issue form be in use?

185. Have you been able to easily identify success criteria and create objective measurements for each of the Social Data project scopes goal statements?

186. Are there specific processes you will use to evaluate and approve/reject changes?

187. Elements that deal with providing the detail?

188. Were key Social Data project stakeholders brought into the Social Data project Plan?

189. Will there be a Change Control Process in place?

190. What is change?

191. Will the risk plan be updated on a regular and frequent basis?

192. What is the most common tool for helping define the detail?

193. Why do you need to manage scope?

194. Has everyone approved the Social Data projects scope statement?

195. Will you need a statement of work?

196. Does the scope statement still need some clarity?

197. Is the Social Data project sponsor function identified and defined?

198. Elements of scope management that deal with concept development ?

2.7 Assumption and Constraint Log: Social Data

199. What strengths do you have?

200. Do you know what your customers expectations are regarding this process?

201. Are funding and staffing resource estimates sufficiently detailed and documented for use in planning and tracking the Social Data project?

202. What do you audit?

203. Have the scope, objectives, costs, benefits and impacts been communicated to all involved and/or impacted stakeholders and work groups?

204. Does the plan conform to standards?

205. Has a Social Data project Communications Plan been developed?

206. How can constraints be violated?

207. How relevant is this attribute to this Social Data project or audit?

208. Does the traceability documentation describe the tool and/or mechanism to be used to capture traceability throughout the life cycle?

209. Is this model reasonable?

210. Is the definition of the Social Data project scope clear; what needs to be accomplished?

211. Are there procedures in place to effectively manage interdependencies with other Social Data projects / systems?

212. Are there cosmetic errors that hinder readability and comprehension?

213. What other teams / processes would be impacted by changes to the current process, and how?

214. Would known impacts serve as impediments?

215. Does a specific action and/or state that is known to violate security policy occur?

216. How can you prevent/fix violations?

217. Are processes for release management of new development from coding and unit testing, to integration testing, to training, and production defined and followed?

218. Is the steering committee active in Social Data project oversight?

2.8 Work Breakdown Structure: Social Data

219. Do you need another level?

220. Why would you develop a Work Breakdown Structure?

221. Who has to do it?

222. Where does it take place?

223. What is the probability of completing the Social Data project in less that xx days?

224. What is the probability that the Social Data project duration will exceed xx weeks?

225. How much detail?

226. Is it a change in scope?

227. Can you make it?

228. What has to be done?

229. When does it have to be done?

230. How many levels?

231. When do you stop?

232. When would you develop a Work Breakdown

Structure?

233. Is it still viable?

234. How big is a work-package?

2.9 WBS Dictionary: Social Data

235. Does the contractors system provide unit or lot costs when applicable?

236. Does the scheduling system provide for the identification of work progress against technical and other milestones, and also provide for forecasts of completion dates of scheduled work?

237. Are data being used by managers in an effective manner to ascertain Social Data project or functional status, to identify reasons or significant variance, and to initiate appropriate corrective action?

238. Is all budget available as management reserve identified and excluded from the performance measurement baseline?

239. Is cost and schedule performance measurement done in a consistent, systematic manner?

240. Changes in the current direct and Social Data projected base?

241. Are the contractors estimates of costs at completion reconcilable with cost data reported to us?

242. Wbs elements contractually specified for reporting of status to you (lowest level only)?

243. Are control accounts opened and closed based on the start and completion of work contained

therein?

244. Contractor financial periods; for example, annual?

245. Are retroactive changes to direct costs and indirect costs prohibited except for the correction of errors and routine accounting adjustments?

246. Are your organizations and items of cost assigned to each pool identified?

247. Are records maintained to show full accountability for all material purchased for the contract, including the residual inventory?

248. Do work packages reflect the actual way in which the work will be done and are they meaningful products or management-oriented subdivisions of a higher level element of work?

249. What is wrong with this Social Data project?

250. Changes in the nature of the overhead requirements?

251. Is work properly classified as measured effort, LOE, or apportioned effort and appropriately separated?

252. Are internal budgets for authorized, and not priced changes based on the contractors resource plan for accomplishing the work?

253. Are the wbs and organizational levels for application of the Social Data projected overhead

costs identified?

2.10 Schedule Management Plan: Social Data

254. Are there any activities or deliverables being added or gold-plated that could be dropped or scaled back without falling short of the original requirement?

255. Do Social Data project teams & team members report on status / activities / progress?

256. Does the Social Data project have quality set of schedule BOEs?

257. Are the predecessor and successor relationships accurate?

258. Where is the scheduling tool and who has access to it to view it?

259. Is a payment system in place with proper reviews and approvals?

260. Is there any form of automated support for Issues Management?

261. Has the budget been baselined?

262. Who is responsible for estimating the activity durations?

263. Is there an on-going process in place to monitor Social Data project risks?

264. Is documentation created for communication with the suppliers and Vendors?

265. Are the activity durations realistic and at an appropriate level of detail for effective management?

266. Have all unresolved risks been documented?

267. Are internal Social Data project status meetings held at reasonable intervals?

268. Cost / benefit analysis?

269. Has a provision been made to reassess Social Data project risks at various Social Data project stages?

270. Is there an onboarding process in place?

271. Was the scope definition used in task sequencing?

272. Is funded schedule margin reasonable and logically distributed?

273. Has a resource management plan been created?

2.11 Activity List: Social Data

274. How much slack is available in the Social Data project?

275. Where will it be performed?

276. Who will perform the work?

277. Can you determine the activity that must finish, before this activity can start?

278. What are the critical bottleneck activities?

279. What is your organizations history in doing similar activities?

280. What went well?

281. How should ongoing costs be monitored to try to keep the Social Data project within budget?

282. What will be performed?

283. When will the work be performed?

284. How can the Social Data project be displayed graphically to better visualize the activities?

285. What are you counting on?

286. For other activities, how much delay can be tolerated?

287. Are the required resources available or need to be acquired?

288. How detailed should a Social Data project get?

289. How will it be performed?

290. When do the individual activities need to start and finish?

291. How difficult will it be to do specific activities on this Social Data project?

292. Is infrastructure setup part of your Social Data project?

2.12 Activity Attributes: Social Data

293. Which method produces the more accurate cost assignment?

294. How many resources do you need to complete the work scope within a limit of X number of days?

295. Time for overtime?

296. Has management defined a definite timeframe for the turnaround or Social Data project window?

297. How difficult will it be to do specific activities on this Social Data project?

298. Activity: what is Missing?

299. What activity do you think you should spend the most time on?

300. Resource is assigned to?

301. How much activity detail is required?

302. Activity: fair or not fair?

303. Have constraints been applied to the start and finish milestones for the phases?

304. Can more resources be added?

305. What is the general pattern here?

306. Are the required resources available?

307. What is missing?

308. Can you re-assign any activities to another resource to resolve an over-allocation?

2.13 Milestone List: Social Data

309. Sustaining internal capabilities?

310. Gaps in capabilities?

311. Do you foresee any technical risks or developmental challenges?

312. How late can the activity start?

313. Which path is the critical path?

314. Own known vulnerabilities?

315. Obstacles faced?

316. Who will manage the Social Data project on a day-to-day basis?

317. Competitive advantages?

318. How do you manage time?

319. Timescales, deadlines and pressures?

320. It is to be a narrative text providing the crucial aspects of your Social Data project proposal answering what, who, how, when and where?

321. Vital contracts and partners?

322. Effects on core activities, distraction?

323. Political effects?

324. Loss of key staff?

2.14 Network Diagram: Social Data

325. Where do schedules come from?

326. Can you calculate the confidence level?

327. Where do you schedule uncertainty time?

328. What are the Major Administrative Issues?

329. What must be completed before an activity can be started?

330. Which type of network diagram allows you to depict four types of dependencies?

331. Are the gantt chart and/or network diagram updated periodically and used to assess the overall Social Data project timetable?

332. If x is long, what would be the completion time if you break x into two parallel parts of y weeks and z weeks?

333. What job or jobs could run concurrently?

334. How difficult will it be to do specific activities on this Social Data project?

335. What activities must occur simultaneously with this activity?

336. Planning: who, how long, what to do?

337. What to do and When?

338. What is the completion time?

339. Why must you schedule milestones, such as reviews, throughout the Social Data project?

340. What activity must be completed immediately before this activity can start?

341. If the Social Data project network diagram cannot change and you have extra personnel resources, what is the BEST thing to do?

342. What is the probability of completing the Social Data project in less that xx days?

2.15 Activity Resource Requirements: Social Data

343. What is the Work Plan Standard?

344. How many signatures do you require on a check and does this match what is in your policy and procedures?

345. What are constraints that you might find during the Human Resource Planning process?

346. Which logical relationship does the PDM use most often?

347. Anything else?

348. Organizational Applicability?

349. Are there unresolved issues that need to be addressed?

350. Do you use tools like decomposition and rolling-wave planning to produce the activity list and other outputs?

351. Is there anything planned that does not need to be here?

352. Other support in specific areas?

353. Why do you do that?

354. How do you handle petty cash?

355. When does monitoring begin?

2.16 Resource Breakdown Structure: Social Data

356. What defines a successful Social Data project?

357. Which resources should be in the resource pool?

358. How difficult will it be to do specific activities on this Social Data project?

359. Why do you do it?

360. Any changes from stakeholders?

361. What is the primary purpose of the human resource plan?

362. What is each stakeholders desired outcome for the Social Data project?

363. When do they need the information?

364. What is the number one predictor of a groups productivity?

365. What are the requirements for resource data?

366. What is the purpose of assigning and documenting responsibility?

367. Why is this important?

368. What defines a successful Social Data project?

369. What is the difference between % Complete and % work?

370. How should the information be delivered?

2.17 Activity Duration Estimates: Social Data

371. What are crucial elements of successful Social Data project plan execution?

372. Is a standard form used to obtain bids and proposals from prospective sellers?

373. Social Data project has three critical paths. Which BEST describes how this affects the Social Data project?

374. Who has the PRIMARY responsibility to solve this problem?

375. Social Data project manager is using weighted average duration estimates to perform schedule network analysis. Which type of mathematical analysis is being used?

376. Are actual Social Data project results compared with planned or expected results to determine the variance?

377. Is the cost performance monitored to identify variances from the plan?

378. Are contractor costs, schedule and technical performance monitored throughout the Social Data project?

379. Are Social Data project activities decomposed

into manageable components to ensure expected management control?

380. Consider the common sources of risk on information technology Social Data projects and suggestions for managing them. Which suggestions do you find most useful?

381. What are the main types of contracts if you do decide to outsource?

382. What type of activity sequencing method is required for corresponding activities?

383. Are Social Data project results verified and Social Data project documents archived?

384. If the optimiztic estimate for an activity is 12days, and the pessimistic estimate is 18days, what is the standard deviation of this activity?

385. How does the job market and current state of the economy affect human resource management?

386. What is the shortest possible time it will take to complete this Social Data project?

387. What is done after activity duration estimation?

388. What steps did your organization take to earn this prestigious quality award?

389. How does poking fun at technical professionals communications skills impact the industry and educational programs?

2.18 Duration Estimating Worksheet: Social Data

390. What is an Average Social Data project?

391. Science = process: remember the scientific method?

392. When, then?

393. What utility impacts are there?

394. Is the Social Data project responsive to community need?

395. What is next?

396. Define the work as completely as possible. What work will be included in the Social Data project?

397. What is your role?

398. What work will be included in the Social Data project?

399. Do any colleagues have experience with your organization and/or RFPs?

400. Can the Social Data project be constructed as planned?

401. Is this operation cost effective?

402. How should ongoing costs be monitored to try to keep the Social Data project within budget?

403. How can the Social Data project be displayed graphically to better visualize the activities?

404. Is a construction detail attached (to aid in explanation)?

405. Why estimate time and cost?

406. Done before proceeding with this activity or what can be done concurrently?

2.19 Project Schedule: Social Data

407. Your Social Data project management plan results in a Social Data project schedule that is too long. If the Social Data project network diagram cannot change and you have extra personnel resources, what is the BEST thing to do?

408. Activity charts and bar charts are graphical representations of a Social Data project schedule ...how do they differ?

409. Are there activities that came from a template or previous Social Data project that are not applicable on this phase of this Social Data project?

410. Was the Social Data project schedule reviewed by all stakeholders and formally accepted?

411. Have all Social Data project delays been adequately accounted for, communicated to all stakeholders and adjustments made in overall Social Data project schedule?

412. How do you know that youhave done this right?

413. Does the condition or event threaten the Social Data projects objectives in any ways?

414. Change management required?

415. It allows the Social Data project to be delivered on schedule. How Do you Use Schedules?

416. Are the original Social Data project schedule and budget realistic?

417. How can you fix it?

418. How can you minimize or control changes to Social Data project schedules?

419. How do you manage Social Data project Risk?

420. What is the most mis-scheduled part of process?

421. Month Social Data project take?

422. What is the purpose of a Social Data project schedule?

423. Should you include sub-activities?

424. Understand the constraints used in preparing the schedule. Are activities connected because logic dictates the order in which others occur?

2.20 Cost Management Plan: Social Data

425. Risk Analysis?

426. Has your organization readiness assessment been conducted?

427. Timeline and milestones?

428. Cost tracking and performance analysis – How will cost tracking and performance analysis be accomplished?

429. Are Social Data project contact logs kept up to date?

430. Are post milestone Social Data project reviews (PMPR) conducted with your organization at least once a year?

431. Does the schedule include Social Data project management time and change request analysis time?

432. The definition of the Social Data project scope what needs to be accomplished?

433. Escalation criteria met?

434. Time management – how will the schedule impact of changes be estimated and approved?

435. What are the Social Data project objectives?

436. Does all Social Data project documentation reside in a common repository for easy access?

437. Schedule variances – how will schedule variances be identified and corrected?

438. Is the Social Data project sponsor clearly communicating the business case or rationale for why this Social Data project is needed?

439. Are assumptions being identified, recorded, analyzed, qualified and closed?

440. Has the scope management document been updated and distributed to help prevent scope creep?

441. Are vendor invoices audited for accuracy before payment?

442. Is it a Social Data project?

443. Is there a formal process for updating the Social Data project baseline?

444. Alignment to strategic goals & objectives?

2.21 Activity Cost Estimates: Social Data

445. How do you treat administrative costs in the activity inventory?

446. Performance bond should always provide what part of the contract value?

447. What areas does the group agree are the biggest success on the Social Data project?

448. Can you delete activities or make them inactive?

449. How many activities should you have?

450. How do you fund change orders?

451. What is included in indirect cost being allocated?

452. How difficult will it be to do specific tasks on the Social Data project?

453. What are the audit requirements?

454. Review – what are some common errors in activities to avoid?

455. What procedures are put in place regarding bidding and cost comparisons, if any?

456. What is the activity inventory?

457. One way to define activities is to consider how organization employees describe jobs to families and friends. You basically want to know, What do you do?

458. Did the consultant work with local staff to develop local capacity?

459. What skill level is required to do the job?

460. Does the estimator have experience?

461. How do you change activities?

462. What makes a good expected result statement?

463. Can you change your activities?

2.22 Cost Estimating Worksheet: Social Data

464. Identify the timeframe necessary to monitor progress and collect data to determine how the selected measure has changed?

465. What is the purpose of estimating?

466. Can a trend be established from historical performance data on the selected measure and are the criteria for using trend analysis or forecasting methods met?

467. Who is best positioned to know and assist in identifying corresponding factors?

468. How will the results be shared and to whom?

469. What costs are to be estimated?

470. What info is needed?

471. Will the Social Data project collaborate with the local community and leverage resources?

472. What is the estimated labor cost today based upon this information?

473. What happens to any remaining funds not used?

474. Does the Social Data project provide innovative ways for stakeholders to overcome obstacles or

deliver better outcomes?

475. What can be included?

476. What additional Social Data project(s) could be initiated as a result of this Social Data project?

477. Is the Social Data project responsive to community need?

478. Is it feasible to establish a control group arrangement?

479. Value pocket identification & quantification what are value pockets?

480. What will others want?

481. Ask: are others positioned to know, are others credible, and will others cooperate?

2.23 Cost Baseline: Social Data

482. Should a more thorough impact analysis be conducted?

483. How likely is it to go wrong?

484. Impact to environment?

485. On time?

486. Review your risk triggers -have your risks changed?

487. Have all approved changes to the schedule baseline been identified and impact on the Social Data project documented?

488. How long are you willing to wait before you find out were late?

489. Has the documentation relating to operation and maintenance of the product(s) or service(s) been delivered to, and accepted by, operations management?

490. Will the Social Data project fail if the change request is not executed?

491. Are procedures defined by which the cost baseline may be changed?

492. What can go wrong?

493. Has the appropriate access to relevant data and analysis capability been granted?

494. Vac -variance at completion, how much over/under budget do you expect to be?

495. What does a good WBS NOT look like?

496. What is the most important thing to do next to make your Social Data project successful?

497. Who will use corresponding metrics ?

498. What deliverables come first?

2.24 Quality Management Plan: Social Data

499. How are your organizations compensation and recognition approaches and the performance management system used to reinforce high performance?

500. How does your organization design processes to ensure others meet customer and others requirements?

501. How are changes approved?

502. How does the material compare to a regulatory threshold?

503. You know what your customers expectations are regarding this process?

504. How are training records kept?

505. Checking the completeness and appropriateness of the sampling and testing. Were the right locations/samples tested for the right parameters?

506. List your organizations customer contact standards that employees are expected to maintain. How are corresponding standards measured?

507. Documented results available?

508. Does the program use modeling in the

permitting or decision-making processes?

509. What are your organizations current levels and trends for the already stated measures related to customer satisfaction/ dissatisfaction and product/ service performance?

510. What data do you gather/use/compile?

511. With the five whys method, the team considers why the issue being explored occurred. do others then take that initial answer and ask why?

512. How do you field-modify testing procedures?

513. What has the QM Collaboration done?

514. What procedures are used to determine if you use, and the number of split, replicate or duplicate samples taken at a site?

515. What are your key performance measures/ indicators for tracking progress relative to your action plans?

516. How do senior leaders create and communicate values and performance expectations?

517. Are there ways to reduce the time it takes to get something approved?

518. Who is responsible for approving the qapp?

2.25 Quality Metrics: Social Data

519. How do you calculate corresponding metrics?

520. Is quality culture a competitive advantage?

521. Has risk analysis been adequately reviewed?

522. How do you measure?

523. There are many reasons to shore up quality-related metrics, and what metrics are important?

524. What happens if you get an abnormal result?

525. If the defect rate during testing is substantially higher than that of the previous release (or a similar product), then ask: Did you plan for and actually improve testing effectiveness?

526. Do the operators focus on determining; is there anything you need to worry about?

527. Was the overall quality better or worse than previous products?

528. Were number of defects identified?

529. Was material distributed on time?

530. What level of statistical confidence do you use?

531. Filter visualizations of interest?

532. Are quality metrics defined?

533. What is the timeline to meet your goal?

534. What approved evidence based screening tools can be used?

535. What is the CMS Benchmark?

536. Product Availability ?

537. Which report did you use to create the data you are submitting?

2.26 Process Improvement Plan: Social Data

538. Does your process ensure quality?

539. Purpose of goal: the motive is determined by asking, why do you want to achieve this goal?

540. Everyone agrees on what process improvement is, right?

541. Are you making progress on the goals?

542. What lessons have you learned so far?

543. Are you meeting the quality standards?

544. Have storage and access mechanisms and procedures been determined?

545. What is the test-cycle concept?

546. Management commitment at all levels?

547. What is the return on investment?

548. Are you following the quality standards?

549. Who should prepare the process improvement action plan?

550. Are you making progress on the improvement framework?

551. What personnel are the change agents for your initiative?

552. Have the supporting tools been developed or acquired?

553. If a process improvement framework is being used, which elements will help the problems and goals listed?

554. Where do you want to be?

555. Modeling current processes is great, and will you ever see a return on that investment?

556. Why quality management?

2.27 Responsibility Assignment Matrix: Social Data

557. Too many as: does a proper segregation of duties exist?

558. What do you do when people do not respond?

559. Actual cost of work performed?

560. What is the business need?

561. Are records maintained to show how management reserves are used?

562. With too many people labeled as doing the work, are there too many hands involved?

563. Are data elements reconcilable between internal summary reports and reports forwarded to stakeholders?

564. Is the entire contract planned in time-phased control accounts to the extent practicable?

565. How do you assist them to be as productive as possible?

566. Identify potential or actual budget-based and time-based schedule variances?

567. Are management actions taken to reduce indirect costs when there are significant adverse

variances?

568. Is budgeted cost for work performed calculated in a manner consistent with the way work is planned?

569. Does a missing responsibility indicate that the current Social Data project is not yet fully understood?

570. Are people encouraged to bring up issues?

571. Is all contract work included in the CWBS?

572. Contemplated overhead expenditure for each period based on the best information currently available?

2.28 Roles and Responsibilities: Social Data

573. What is working well?

574. Attainable / achievable: the goal is attainable; can you actually accomplish the goal?

575. How is your work-life balance?

576. What should you do now to prepare yourself for a promotion, increased responsibilities or a different job?

577. What should you highlight for improvement?

578. Does the team have access to and ability to use data analysis tools?

579. Where are you most strong as a supervisor?

580. How well did the Social Data project Team understand the expectations of specific roles and responsibilities?

581. Are Social Data project team roles and responsibilities identified and documented?

582. Is there a training program in place for stakeholders covering expectations, roles and responsibilities and any addition knowledge others need to be good stakeholders?

583. Required skills, knowledge, experience?

584. Is feedback clearly communicated and non-judgmental?

585. Key conclusions and recommendations: Are conclusions and recommendations relevant and acceptable?

586. Are governance roles and responsibilities documented?

587. Who is responsible for each task?

588. What specific behaviors did you observe?

589. What expectations were NOT met?

590. Are the quality assurance functions and related roles and responsibilities clearly defined?

2.29 Human Resource Management Plan: Social Data

591. Are the results of quality assurance reviews provided to affected groups & individuals?

592. Is quality monitored from the perspective of the customers needs and expectations?

593. Are risk oriented checklists used during risk identification?

594. Has a structured approach been used to break work effort into manageable components (WBS)?

595. Are issues raised, assessed, actioned, and resolved in a timely and efficient manner?

596. Is Social Data project work proceeding in accordance with the original Social Data project schedule?

597. Are decisions captured in a decisions log?

598. Have all involved Social Data project stakeholders and work groups committed to the Social Data project?

599. Has a provision been made to reassess Social Data project risks at various Social Data project stages?

600. Have key stakeholders been identified?

601. Were stakeholders aware and supportive of the principles and practices of modern cost estimation?

602. Is Social Data project status reviewed with the steering and executive teams at appropriate intervals?

603. Have all necessary approvals been obtained?

604. How will the Social Data project manage expectations & meet needs and requirements?

605. Are trade-offs between accepting the risk and mitigating the risk identified?

606. Personnel with expertise?

607. Are non-critical path items updated and agreed upon with the teams?

608. Were Social Data project team members involved in detailed estimating and scheduling?

609. How complete is the human resource management plan?

2.30 Communications Management Plan: Social Data

610. What data is going to be required?

611. Which stakeholders are thought leaders, influences, or early adopters?

612. Who to learn from?

613. Why do you manage communications?

614. Do you feel more overwhelmed by stakeholders?

615. Who did you turn to if you had questions?

616. Is the stakeholder role recognized by your organization?

617. Are there common objectives between the team and the stakeholder?

618. Which team member will work with each stakeholder?

619. Why is stakeholder engagement important?

620. What does the stakeholder need from the team?

621. Do you have members of your team responsible for certain stakeholders?

622. Do you then often overlook a key stakeholder or

stakeholder group?

623. How often do you engage with stakeholders?

624. Who will use or be affected by the result of a Social Data project?

625. How did the term stakeholder originate?

626. What is the stakeholders level of authority?

627. Who is responsible?

628. How do you manage communications?

629. Who have you worked with in past, similar initiatives?

2.31 Risk Management Plan: Social Data

630. Management -what contingency plans do you have if the risk becomes a reality?

631. What risks are tracked?

632. Do requirements demand the use of new analysis, design, or testing methods?

633. Are the metrics meaningful and useful?

634. Is Social Data project scope stable?

635. How quickly does this item need to be resolved?

636. Where are you confronted with risks during the business phases?

637. Are testing tools available and suitable?

638. Have staff received necessary training?

639. My Social Data project leader has suddenly left your organization, what do you do?

640. How do you manage Social Data project Risk?

641. Are you working on the right risks?

642. What are the chances the event will occur?

643. Degree of confidence in estimated size estimate?

644. Has something like this been done before?

645. What is the cost to the Social Data project if it does occur?

646. Are some people working on multiple Social Data projects?

647. Have top software and customer managers formally committed to support the Social Data project?

648. People risk -are people with appropriate skills available to help complete the Social Data project?

649. How risk averse are you?

2.32 Risk Register: Social Data

650. What may happen or not go according to plan?

651. Who is going to do it?

652. What are the assumptions and current status that support the assessment of the risk?

653. How is a Community Risk Register created?

654. Are there any gaps in the evidence?

655. What is the probability and impact of the risk occurring?

656. Amongst the action plans and recommendations that you have to introduce are there some that could stop or delay the overall program?

657. Are there other alternative controls that could be implemented?

658. What evidence do you have to justify the likelihood score of the risk (audit, incident report, claim, complaints, inspection, internal review)?

659. Do you require further engagement?

660. How could corresponding Risk affect the Social Data project in terms of cost and schedule?

661. What are you going to do to limit the Social Data projects risk exposure due to the identified risks?

662. Contingency actions - planned actions to reduce the immediate seriousness of the risk when it does occur. What should you do when?

663. Are implemented controls working as others should?

664. What is a Risk?

665. Budget and schedule: what are the estimated costs and schedules for performing risk-related activities?

666. What are the major risks facing the Social Data project?

667. Severity Prediction?

668. What can be done about it?

669. Who is accountable?

2.33 Probability and Impact Assessment: Social Data

670. Assuming that you have identified a number of risks in the Social Data project, how would you prioritize them?

671. What things are likely to change?

672. Are requirements fully understood by the software engineering team and customers?

673. Anticipated volatility of the requirements?

674. Risks should be identified during which phase of Social Data project management life cycle?

675. What should be the requirement of organizational restructuring as each subSocial Data project goes through a different lifecycle phase?

676. Are formal technical reviews part of this process?

677. Can it be enlarged by drawing people from other areas of your organization?

678. What are the likely future requirements?

679. What are the probabilities of chosen technologies being suitable for local conditions?

680. Is the number of people on the Social Data project team adequate to do the job?

681. Do you use any methods to analyze risks?

682. How do you define a risk?

683. What are its business ethics?

684. What is the likely future demand of the customer?

685. Are the best people available?

686. Do end-users have realistic expectations?

687. How is the Social Data project going to be managed?

688. What new technologies are being explored in the same area?

2.34 Probability and Impact Matrix: Social Data

689. How realistic is the timing of introduction?

690. Does the software engineering team have the right mix of skills?

691. What changes in the regulation are forthcoming?

692. How would you suggest monitoring for risk transition indicators?

693. Pay attention to the quality of the plans: is the content complete, or does it seem to be lacking detail?

694. Are you on schedule?

695. What needs to be DONE?

696. What are ways to measure and evaluate risks?

697. Is the number of people on the Social Data project team adequate to do the job?

698. Do requirements put excessive performance constraints on the product?

699. Which of the risk factors can be avoided altogether?

700. Are tools for analysis and design available?

701. Do you train all developers in the process?

702. What is the culture of the market and your organization?

703. What will the damage be?

704. How carefully have the potential competitors been identified?

705. What are the current requirements of the customer?

706. Are Social Data project requirements stable?

707. What is the level of commitment and professionalism?

2.35 Risk Data Sheet: Social Data

708. Do effective diagnostic tests exist?

709. What is the chance that it will happen?

710. What can you do?

711. What is the environment within which you operate (social trends, economic, community values, broad based participation, national directions etc.)?

712. What do people affected think about the need for, and practicality of preventive measures?

713. What were the Causes that contributed?

714. Will revised controls lead to tolerable risk levels?

715. During work activities could hazards exist?

716. Whom do you serve (customers)?

717. How reliable is the data source?

718. Has a sensitivity analysis been carried out?

719. What are you weak at and therefore need to do better?

720. What will be the consequences if it happens?

721. How can hazards be reduced?

722. Are new hazards created?

723. If it happens, what are the consequences?

724. What are you trying to achieve (Objectives)?

725. What are the main threats to your existence?

726. What can happen?

2.36 Procurement Management Plan: Social Data

727. Has the Social Data project scope been baselined?

728. Is stakeholder involvement adequate?

729. Do Social Data project teams & team members report on status / activities / progress?

730. Is there a procurement management plan in place?

731. Is the quality assurance team identified?

732. How will the duration of the Social Data project influence your decisions?

733. Are status reports received per the Social Data project Plan?

734. Are action items captured and managed?

735. What is the last item a Social Data project manager must do to finalize Social Data project close-out?

736. Are schedule deliverables actually delivered?

737. Is the structure for tracking the Social Data project schedule well defined and assigned to a specific individual?

738. Does the Social Data project team have the right skills?

739. Were escalated issues resolved promptly?

740. Public engagement – did you get it right?

741. Was an original risk assessment/risk management plan completed?

742. Are risk triggers captured?

2.37 Source Selection Criteria: Social Data

743. What documentation is needed for a tradeoff decision?

744. Do you consider all weaknesses, significant weaknesses, and deficiencies?

745. Is the contracting office likely to receive more purchase requests for this item or service during the coming year?

746. Are there any specific considerations that precludes offers from being selected as the awardee?

747. In which phase of the acquisition process cycle does source qualifications reside?

748. What management structure does your organization consider as optimal for performing the contract?

749. Who should attend debriefings?

750. If the costs are normalized, please account for how the normalization is conducted. Is a cost realism analysis used?

751. What should communications be used to accomplish?

752. Do you have designated specific forms or

worksheets?

753. What should be the contracting officers strategy?

754. How should comments received in response to a RFP be handled?

755. How do you ensure an integrated assessment of proposals?

756. What will you use to capture evaluation and subsequent documentation?

757. What is price analysis and when should it be performed?

758. How should the solicitation aspects regarding past performance be structured?

759. Can you make a cost/technical tradeoff?

760. Do you want to have them collaborate at subfactor level?

761. Which contract type places the most risk on the seller?

762. What risks were identified in the proposals?

2.38 Stakeholder Management Plan: Social Data

763. Does the business case include how the Social Data project aligns with your organizations strategic goals & objectives?

764. Are multiple estimation methods being employed?

765. Does the role of the Social Data project Team cease upon the delivery of the Social Data projects outputs?

766. Are there processes in place to ensure internal consistency between the source code components?

767. Has the business need been clearly defined?

768. Is there a formal set of procedures supporting Issues Management?

769. Are the appropriate IT resources adequate to meet planned commitments?

770. Contradictory information between different documents?

771. Are changes in deliverable commitments agreed to by all affected groups & individuals?

772. Are meeting minutes captured and sent out after the meeting?

773. What records are required (eg purchase orders, agreements)?

774. Is the process working, and are people executing in compliance of the process?

775. Do all stakeholders know how to access this repository and where to find the Social Data project documentation?

776. Does the Social Data project have a Quality Culture?

777. Is the assigned Social Data project manager a PMP (Certified Social Data project manager) and experienced?

778. Are vendor contract reports, reviews and visits conducted periodically?

2.39 Change Management Plan: Social Data

779. Will the culture embrace or reject this change?

780. Why is the initiative is being undertaken - What are the business drivers?

781. Has an information & communications plan been developed?

782. What work practices will be affected?

783. Have the business unit contacts been briefed by the Social Data project team?

784. Who might be able to help you the most?

785. What are the needs, priorities and special interests of the audience?

786. Do the proposed users have access to the appropriate documentation?

787. What are the training strategies?

788. What processes are in place to manage knowledge about the Social Data project?

789. Has the training provider been established?

790. What prerequisite knowledge or training is required?

791. Who should be involved in developing a change management strategy?

792. What is going to be done differently?

793. What policies and procedures need to be changed?

794. What risks may occur upfront?

795. Who will be the change levers?

796. Is there a support model for this application and are the details available for distribution?

797. What did the people around you say about it?

3.0 Executing Process Group: Social Data

798. Would you rate yourself as being risk-averse, risk-neutral, or risk-seeking?

799. How well did the chosen processes fit the needs of the Social Data project?

800. How do you enter durations, link tasks, and view critical path information?

801. How is Social Data project performance information created and distributed?

802. Is the Social Data project making progress in helping to achieve the set results?

803. Do schedule issues conflicts?

804. Who will be the main sponsor?

805. Are the necessary foundations in place to ensure the sustainability of the results of the programme?

806. Will new hardware or software be required for servers or client machines?

807. What areas does the group agree are the biggest success on the Social Data project?

808. What are deliverables of your Social Data project?

809. Who will provide training?

810. How does Social Data project management relate to other disciplines?

811. What factors are contributing to progress or delay in the achievement of products and results?

812. How do you measure difficulty?

813. How do you prevent staff are just doing busywork to pass the time?

814. What is the critical path for this Social Data project and how long is it?

815. Could a new application negatively affect the current IT infrastructure?

3.1 Team Member Status Report: Social Data

816. How it is to be done?

817. Will the staff do training or is that done by a third party?

818. What is to be done?

819. Does the product, good, or service already exist within your organization?

820. The problem with Reward & Recognition Programs is that the truly deserving people all too often get left out. How can you make it practical?

821. How will resource planning be done?

822. Does your organization have the means (staff, money, contract, etc.) to produce or to acquire the product, good, or service?

823. Why is it to be done?

824. Are your organizations Social Data projects more successful over time?

825. When a teams productivity and success depend on collaboration and the efficient flow of information, what generally fails them?

826. Do you have an Enterprise Social Data project

Management Office (EPMO)?

827. Are the products of your organizations Social Data projects meeting customers objectives?

828. Are the attitudes of staff regarding Social Data project work improving?

829. What specific interest groups do you have in place?

830. Is there evidence that staff is taking a more professional approach toward management of your organizations Social Data projects?

831. How does this product, good, or service meet the needs of the Social Data project and your organization as a whole?

832. How can you make it practical?

833. Does every department have to have a Social Data project Manager on staff?

834. How much risk is involved?

3.2 Change Request: Social Data

835. Are change requests logged and managed?

836. Who will perform the change?

837. Who is responsible for the implementation and monitoring of all measures?

838. Will all change requests and current status be logged?

839. Why control change across the life cycle?

840. What is the relationship between requirements attributes and attributes like complexity and size?

841. How shall the implementation of changes be recorded?

842. Who has responsibility for approving and ranking changes?

843. Are there requirements attributes that are strongly related to the complexity and size?

844. Can static requirements change attributes like the size of the change be used to predict reliability in execution?

845. What should be regulated in a change control operating instruction?

846. What kind of information about the change

request needs to be captured?

847. What are the Impacts to your organization?

848. How are the measures for carrying out the change established?

849. Has the change been highlighted and documented in the CSCI?

850. Who is included in the change control team?

851. What are the duties of the change control team?

852. What is the purpose of change control?

853. How do team members communicate with each other?

854. Who is responsible to authorize changes?

3.3 Change Log: Social Data

855. When was the request approved?

856. Will the Social Data project fail if the change request is not executed?

857. When was the request submitted?

858. Does the suggested change request seem to represent a necessary enhancement to the product?

859. Do the described changes impact on the integrity or security of the system?

860. Is the change request open, closed or pending?

861. Where do changes come from?

862. How does this change affect the timeline of the schedule?

863. Is the submitted change a new change or a modification of a previously approved change?

864. Is the requested change request a result of changes in other Social Data project(s)?

865. Who initiated the change request?

866. Is this a mandatory replacement?

867. How does this change affect scope?

868. Is the change request within Social Data project scope?

869. Does the suggested change request represent a desired enhancement to the products functionality?

870. How does this relate to the standards developed for specific business processes?

871. Is the change backward compatible without limitations?

3.4 Decision Log: Social Data

872. What was the rationale for the decision?

873. Who is the decisionmaker?

874. How effective is maintaining the log at facilitating organizational learning?

875. At what point in time does loss become unacceptable?

876. What is the line where eDiscovery ends and document review begins?

877. Who will be given a copy of this document and where will it be kept?

878. What is your overall strategy for quality control / quality assurance procedures?

879. How do you define success?

880. How does an increasing emphasis on cost containment influence the strategies and tactics used?

881. Behaviors; what are guidelines that the team has identified that will assist them with getting the most out of team meetings?

882. How does the use a Decision Support System influence the strategies/tactics or costs?

883. It becomes critical to track and periodically revisit both operational effectiveness; Are you noticing all that you need to, and are you interpreting what you see effectively?

884. What are the cost implications?

885. Is everything working as expected?

886. Meeting purpose; why does this team meet?

887. Adversarial environment. is your opponent open to a non-traditional workflow, or will it likely challenge anything you do?

888. What eDiscovery problem or issue did your organization set out to fix or make better?

889. Does anything need to be adjusted?

890. Decision-making process; how will the team make decisions?

891. What makes you different or better than others companies selling the same thing?

3.5 Quality Audit: Social Data

892. How does your organization know that its general support services planning and management systems are appropriately effective and constructive?

893. Is there a written corporate quality policy?

894. What does the organizarion look for in a Quality audit?

895. Are there appropriate means for intervening if necessary?

896. What are you trying to do?

897. Does the audit organization have experience in performing the required work for entities of your type and size?

898. Is the reports overall tone appropriate?

899. How does your organization know that its systems for communicating with and among staff are appropriately effective and constructive?

900. Does everyone know what they are supposed to be doing, how and why?

901. Statements of intent remain exactly that until they are put into effect. The next step is to deploy the already stated intentions. In other words, do the plans happen in reality?

902. Are all complaints involving the possible failure of a device, labeling, or packaging to meet any of its specifications reviewed, evaluated, and investigated?

903. Have personnel cleanliness and health requirements been established?

904. How does your organization know that its system for supporting staff research capability is appropriately effective and constructive?

905. Is progress against the intentions measurable?

906. Are all areas associated with the storage and reconditioning of devices clean, free of rubbish, adequately ventilated and in good repair?

907. How does your organization know that its system for examining work done is appropriately effective and constructive?

908. What data about organizational performance is routinely collected and reported?

909. If your organization thinks it is doing something well, can it prove this?

910. How does your organization know that the review processes are effective?

911. Are there sufficient personnel having the necessary education, background, training, and experience to assure that all operations are correctly performed?

3.6 Team Directory: Social Data

912. Do purchase specifications and configurations match requirements?

913. Is construction on schedule?

914. Where will the product be used and/or delivered or built when appropriate?

915. Who will write the meeting minutes and distribute?

916. How will the team handle changes?

917. Who are your stakeholders (customers, sponsors, end users, team members)?

918. How does the team resolve conflicts and ensure tasks are completed?

919. Where should the information be distributed?

920. Process decisions: is work progressing on schedule and per contract requirements?

921. Contract requirements complied with?

922. Have you decided when to celebrate the Social Data projects completion date?

923. Timing: when do the effects of communication take place?

924. Who will be the stakeholders on your next Social Data project?

925. Process decisions: how well was task order work performed?

926. How will you accomplish and manage the objectives?

927. Who are the Team Members?

928. Process decisions: which organizational elements and which individuals will be assigned management functions?

3.7 Team Operating Agreement: Social Data

929. Did you prepare participants for the next meeting?

930. Did you draft the meeting agenda?

931. Do you leverage technology engagement tools group chat, polls, screen sharing, etc.?

932. What is the anticipated procedure (recruitment, solicitation of volunteers, or assignment) for selecting team members?

933. Do you begin with a question to engage everyone?

934. Are there more than two native languages represented by your team?

935. What is group supervision?

936. Do you post meeting notes and the recording (if used) and notify participants?

937. What types of accommodations will be formulated and put in place for sustaining the team?

938. Do you send out the agenda and meeting materials in advance?

939. Must your team members rely on the expertise of

other members to complete tasks?

940. What are the safety issues/risks that need to be addressed and/or that the team needs to consider?

941. Do you ask participants to close laptops and place mobile devices on silent on the table while the meeting is in progress?

942. Do you upload presentation materials in advance and test the technology?

943. Do you solicit member feedback about meetings and what would make them better?

944. Why does your organization want to participate in teaming?

945. Do you listen for voice tone and word choice to understand the meaning behind words?

946. Do you post any action items, due dates, and responsibilities on the team website?

947. Do you ensure that all participants know how to use the required technology?

3.8 Team Performance Assessment: Social Data

948. To what degree do team members understand one anothers roles and skills?

949. Can team performance be reliably measured in simulator and live exercises using the same assessment tool?

950. To what degree will the team adopt a concrete, clearly understood, and agreed-upon approach that will result in achievement of the teams goals?

951. Social categorization and intergroup behaviour: Does minimal intergroup discrimination make social identity more positive?

952. To what degree do the goals specify concrete team work products?

953. To what degree are the goals ambitious?

954. To what degree are the members clear on what they are individually responsible for and what they are jointly responsible for?

955. To what degree does the team possess adequate membership to achieve its ends?

956. How do you manage human resources?

957. When a reviewer complains about method

variance, what is the essence of the complaint?

958. To what degree will the approach capitalize on and enhance the skills of all team members in a manner that takes into consideration other demands on members of the team?

959. How do you encourage members to learn from each other?

960. What makes opportunities more or less obvious?

961. To what degree do all members feel responsible for all agreed-upon measures?

962. To what degree can all members engage in open and interactive considerations?

963. How does Social Data project termination impact Social Data project team members?

964. To what degree does the teams work approach provide opportunity for members to engage in open interaction?

965. To what degree are fresh input and perspectives systematically caught and added (for example, through information and analysis, new members, and senior sponsors)?

966. To what degree will team members, individually and collectively, commit time to help themselves and others learn and develop skills?

3.9 Team Member Performance Assessment: Social Data

967. Where can team members go for more detailed information on performance measurement and assessment?

968. To what degree do team members frequently explore the teams purpose and its implications?

969. Did training work?

970. How accurately is your plan implemented?

971. What are the key duties or tasks of the Ratee?

972. To what degree do team members articulate the teams work approach?

973. What is the role of the Reviewer?

974. Do the goals support your organizations goals?

975. What entity leads the process, selects a potential restructuring option and develops the plan?

976. Are any governance changes sufficient to impact achievement?

977. What makes them effective?

978. To what degree will new and supplemental skills be introduced as the need is recognized?

979. How will they be formed?

980. Is there reluctance to join a team?

981. What is used as a basis for instructional decisions?

982. To what degree are the skill areas critical to team performance present?

983. What are the standards or expectations for success?

984. What resources do you need?

985. How often are assessments to be conducted?

986. In what areas would you like to concentrate your knowledge and resources?

3.10 Issue Log: Social Data

987. What effort will a change need?

988. Is there an important stakeholder who is actively opposed and will not receive messages?

989. What approaches do you use?

990. What help do you and your team need from the stakeholders?

991. What date was the issue resolved?

992. Who is the issue assigned to?

993. Who were proponents/opponents?

994. Can an impact cause deviation beyond team, stage or Social Data project tolerances?

995. Is the issue log kept in a safe place?

996. What is the status of the issue?

997. What are the typical contents?

998. What is the impact on the risks?

999. What is a change?

4.0 Monitoring and Controlling Process Group: Social Data

1000. Do the partners have sufficient financial capacity to keep up the benefits produced by the programme?

1001. How well did the chosen processes produce the expected results?

1002. Did it work?

1003. How well did the chosen processes fit the needs of the Social Data project?

1004. Propriety: who needs to be involved in the evaluation to be ethical?

1005. What is the timeline for the Social Data project?

1006. How is agile portfolio management done?

1007. What will you do to minimize the impact should a risk event occur?

1008. Overall, how does the program function to serve the clients?

1009. What do they need to know about the Social Data project?

1010. What is the timeline?

1011. How is Agile Social Data project Management done?

1012. How is agile program management done?

1013. How were collaborations developed, and how are they sustained?

1014. Who are the Social Data project stakeholders?

1015. Is progress on outcomes due to your program?

1016. User: who wants the information and what are they interested in?

1017. Are the services being delivered?

1018. Based on your Social Data project communication management plan, what worked well?

4.1 Project Performance Report: Social Data

1019. How is the data used?

1020. To what degree does the teams purpose constitute a broader, deeper aspiration than just accomplishing short-term goals?

1021. To what degree is the team cognizant of small wins to be celebrated along the way?

1022. To what degree do team members agree with the goals, relative importance, and the ways in which achievement will be measured?

1023. How will procurement be coordinated with other Social Data project aspects, such as scheduling and performance reporting?

1024. To what degree does the information network provide individuals with the information they require?

1025. To what degree does the informal organization make use of individual resources and meet individual needs?

1026. To what degree are the goals realistic?

1027. Next Steps?

1028. To what degree can team members frequently and easily communicate with one another?

1029. To what degree are sub-teams possible or necessary?

1030. To what degree can team members vigorously define the teams purpose in considerations with others who are not part of the functioning team?

1031. To what degree do the relationships of the informal organization motivate taskrelevant behavior and facilitate task completion?

1032. To what degree are the structures of the formal organization consistent with the behaviors in the informal organization?

1033. To what degree can the cognitive capacity of individuals accommodate the flow of information?

4.2 Variance Analysis: Social Data

1034. How are variances affected by multiple material and labor categories?

1035. Is data disseminated to the contractors management timely, accurate, and usable?

1036. What causes selling price variance?

1037. Are all authorized tasks assigned to identified organizational elements?

1038. Can the contractor substantiate work package and planning package budgets?

1039. Are procedures for variance analysis documented and consistently applied at the control account level and selected WBS and organizational levels at least monthly as a routine task?

1040. Other relevant issues of Variance Analysis -selling price or gross margin?

1041. What types of services and expense are shared between business segments?

1042. Historical experience?

1043. How are material, labor, and overhead standards set?

1044. Does the accounting system provide a basis for auditing records of direct costs chargeable to the contract?

1045. Are estimates of costs at completion generated in a rational, consistent manner?

1046. What is the dollar amount of the fluctuation?

1047. Who is generally responsible for monitoring and taking action on variances?

1048. Did an existing competitor change strategy?

1049. What are the direct labor dollars and/or hours?

1050. Does the scheduling system identify in a timely manner the status of work?

1051. What was the cause of the increase in costs?

1052. What is the performance to date and material commitment?

4.3 Earned Value Status: Social Data

1053. How does this compare with other Social Data projects?

1054. Earned value can be used in almost any Social Data project situation and in almost any Social Data project environment. it may be used on large Social Data projects, medium sized Social Data projects, tiny Social Data projects (in cut-down form), complex and simple Social Data projects and in any market sector. some people, of course, know all about earned value, they have used it for years - but perhaps not as effectively as they could have?

1055. Validation is a process of ensuring that the developed system will actually achieve the stakeholders desired outcomes; Are you building the right product? What do you validate?

1056. Where are your problem areas?

1057. If earned value management (EVM) is so good in determining the true status of a Social Data project and Social Data project its completion, why is it that hardly any one uses it in information systems related Social Data projects?

1058. What is the unit of forecast value?

1059. Where is evidence-based earned value in your organization reported?

1060. When is it going to finish?

1061. How much is it going to cost by the finish?

1062. Are you hitting your Social Data projects targets?

1063. Verification is a process of ensuring that the developed system satisfies the stakeholders agreements and specifications; Are you building the product right? What do you verify?

4.4 Risk Audit: Social Data

1064. For paid staff, does your organization comply with the minimum conditions for employment and/or the applicable modern award?

1065. Do you have position descriptions for all key paid and volunteer positions in your organization?

1066. Are enough people available?

1067. Are staff committed for the duration of the product?

1068. To what extent should analytical procedures be utilized in the risk-assessment process?

1069. Have reasonable steps been taken to reduce the risks to acceptable levels?

1070. Does your organization have or has considered the need for insurance covers: public liability, professional indemnity and directors and officers liability?

1071. Who audits the auditor?

1072. What are the legal implications of not identifying a complete universe of business risks?

1073. What is the implication of budget constraint on this process?

1074. How do you prioritize risks?

1075. Do you have an emergency plan?

1076. To what extent are auditors influenced by the business risk assessment in the audit process, and how can auditors create more effective mental models to more fully examine contradictory evidence?

1077. Does your auditor understand your business?

1078. Are there any forms the staff is required to sign?

1079. Do you have written and signed agreements/ contracts in place for each paid staff member?

1080. Do you promote education and training opportunities?

1081. To what extent are auditors effective at linking business risks and management assertions?

1082. Are audit program plans risk-adjusted?

4.5 Contractor Status Report: Social Data

1083. What was the actual budget or estimated cost for your organizations services?

1084. Describe how often regular updates are made to the proposed solution. Are corresponding regular updates included in the standard maintenance plan?

1085. What was the final actual cost?

1086. What was the budget or estimated cost for your organizations services?

1087. How does the proposed individual meet each requirement?

1088. Who can list a Social Data project as organization experience, your organization or a previous employee of your organization?

1089. Are there contractual transfer concerns?

1090. What process manages the contracts?

1091. What was the overall budget or estimated cost?

1092. How long have you been using the services?

1093. If applicable; describe your standard schedule for new software version releases. Are new software version releases included in the standard maintenance plan?

1094. What are the minimum and optimal bandwidth requirements for the proposed solution?

1095. How is risk transferred?

1096. What is the average response time for answering a support call?

4.6 Formal Acceptance: Social Data

1097. What features, practices, and processes proved to be strengths or weaknesses?

1098. Was the Social Data project goal achieved?

1099. Was the client satisfied with the Social Data project results?

1100. What is the Acceptance Management Process?

1101. Who supplies data?

1102. Have all comments been addressed?

1103. Is formal acceptance of the Social Data project product documented and distributed?

1104. What was done right?

1105. How well did the team follow the methodology?

1106. Who would use it?

1107. What function(s) does it fill or meet?

1108. General estimate of the costs and times to complete the Social Data project?

1109. Was business value realized?

1110. Was the Social Data project managed well?

1111. How does your team plan to obtain formal acceptance on your Social Data project?

1112. Did the Social Data project achieve its MOV?

1113. Do you buy pre-configured systems or build your own configuration?

1114. What lessons were learned about your Social Data project management methodology?

1115. Was the Social Data project work done on time, within budget, and according to specification?

1116. What can you do better next time?

5.0 Closing Process Group: Social Data

1117. Will the Social Data project deliverable(s) replace a current asset or group of assets?

1118. Are there funding or time constraints?

1119. Did you do things well?

1120. What areas were overlooked on this Social Data project?

1121. Were cost budgets met?

1122. When will the Social Data project be done?

1123. Did you do what you said you were going to do?

1124. What areas does the group agree are the biggest success on the Social Data project?

1125. How dependent is the Social Data project on other Social Data projects or work efforts?

1126. How critical is the Social Data project success to the success of your organization?

1127. Who are the Social Data project stakeholders?

1128. Were risks identified and mitigated?

1129. What were things that you need to improve?

1130. What level of risk does the proposed budget

represent to the Social Data project?

1131. Did the delivered product meet the specified requirements and goals of the Social Data project?

1132. Does the close educate others to improve performance?

1133. How will you do it?

5.1 Procurement Audit: Social Data

1134. Are procurement processes well organized and documented?

1135. Do you learn from benchmarking your own practices with international standards?

1136. Is there a policy on purchasing from users of organization products?

1137. Is a log maintained over the use of signature plates?

1138. Were no tenders presented after the time limit accepted?

1139. Does the procurement Social Data project comply with European Communities regulations and rules?

1140. Are the right skills, experiences and competencies present in the acquisition workgroup and are the necessary outside specialists involved in part of the process?

1141. Were any additional works or deliveries admissible, without recourse to a new procurement procedure?

1142. Is there a record maintained of the procedures followed in the opening of tenders together with the reasons for the acceptance or rejection of tenders received?

1143. Did the contracting authority draw up a comprehensive written report about progress and outcome of the procurement process?

1144. Has it been determined how large a portion of the procurement portfolio should be managed by the procurement function/unit and how large a portion that should be managed locally?

1145. Are the established budget and timetable (milestones) respected?

1146. Is there no evidence that the consultants participating in the Social Data project design released information to contractors competing for the prime contract?

1147. Are the supporting documents for payments voided or cancelled following payment?

1148. Were the tender documents comprehensive, transparent and non-discriminating?

1149. Are receiving reports on file for all claims for equipment, supplies and materials in the paid claims file?

1150. How do you monitor behaviour of procurement staff?

1151. Are copies of policies made available to staff members involved in budget preparation and administration?

1152. Is there a general policy on approval of

purchases?

1153. In case of time and material and labour hour contracts, does surveillance give an adequate and reasonable assurance that the contractor is using efficient methods and effective cost controls?

5.2 Contract Close-Out: Social Data

1154. Was the contract complete without requiring numerous changes and revisions?

1155. Are the signers the authorized officials?

1156. Change in circumstances?

1157. Was the contract sufficiently clear so as not to result in numerous disputes and misunderstandings?

1158. Change in attitude or behavior?

1159. Was the contract type appropriate?

1160. Parties: Authorized?

1161. What happens to the recipient of services?

1162. Has each contract been audited to verify acceptance and delivery?

1163. Have all contracts been completed?

1164. Have all contract records been included in the Social Data project archives?

1165. Have all contracts been closed?

1166. Change in knowledge?

1167. Have all acceptance criteria been met prior to final payment to contractors?

1168. Why Outsource?

1169. Parties: who is involved?

1170. How does it work?

1171. How is the contracting office notified of the automatic contract close-out?

1172. How/when used ?

1173. What is capture management?

5.3 Project or Phase Close-Out: Social Data

1174. How much influence did the stakeholder have over others?

1175. Was the user/client satisfied with the end product?

1176. What is the information level of detail required for each stakeholder?

1177. Does the lesson educate others to improve performance?

1178. What are they?

1179. What advantages do the an individual interview have over a group meeting, and vice-versa?

1180. In preparing the Lessons Learned report, should it reflect a consensus viewpoint, or should the report reflect the different individual viewpoints?

1181. Were messages directly related to the release strategy or phases of the Social Data project?

1182. Were the outcomes different from the already stated planned?

1183. What are the informational communication needs for each stakeholder?

1184. What was expected from each stakeholder?

1185. What could be done to improve the process?

1186. Which changes might a stakeholder be required to make as a result of the Social Data project?

1187. What process was planned for managing issues/risks?

1188. How often did each stakeholder need an update?

1189. What stakeholder group needs, expectations, and interests are being met by the Social Data project?

1190. Who is responsible for award close-out?

5.4 Lessons Learned: Social Data

1191. Was any formal risk assessment carried out at the start of the Social Data project, and was this followed up during the Social Data project?

1192. What was the single greatest success and the single greatest shortcoming or challenge from the Social Data projects perspective?

1193. Do you have any real problems?

1194. How effective was the training you received in preparation for the use of the product/service?

1195. How actively and meaningfully were stakeholders involved in the Social Data project?

1196. What are the performance measures?

1197. What is the growth stage of your organization?

1198. Where could you improve?

1199. How effective were the techniques used to prepare you and your organization for the impact of the changes brought about by the product or service produced by the Social Data project?

1200. Was the schedule met?

1201. How useful was your testing?

1202. What were the actual outcomes?

1203. Would you spend your own time fixing this issue?

1204. What were the desired outcomes?

1205. How much communication is socially oriented?

1206. What is the frequency of personal communications?

1207. Which estimation issues did you personally have and what was the impact?

1208. Were the Social Data project objectives met (if not, briefly account for what wasnt met)?

1209. Was the necessary hardware, software, accommodation etc available?

Index

ability 37, 85, 189
abnormal 183
acceptable 48, 84, 96, 138-139, 190, 242
acceptance 6, 114, 246-247, 250, 253
accepted 110, 171, 179, 250
accepting 192
access 2, 7-9, 20, 60, 153, 174, 180, 185, 189, 210-211
accomplish 7, 78, 115, 119, 189, 207, 226
accordance 191
according 29, 41, 136, 197, 247
account 27, 49, 207, 238, 258
accounted 171
accounting 151, 238
accounts 150, 187
accrue 135
accuracy 174
accurate 9, 109, 153, 157, 238
accurately 231
achievable 107, 189
achieve 7, 69, 77, 79, 106, 109, 185, 204, 213, 229, 240,
247
achieved 25, 83-84, 117, 246
acquire 215
acquired 156, 186
across 47, 67, 135, 137, 217
action 53, 55, 89-90, 93, 97, 126, 147, 150, 182, 185, 197, 205,
228, 239
actionable 106
actioned 191
actions 16, 89, 92, 118, 187, 198
active 147
actively 233, 257
activities 18, 21-22, 30, 79, 91, 94, 102, 139, 153, 155-159,
161, 165, 167-168, 170-172, 175-176, 198, 203, 205
activity 3-4, 28, 39, 153-155, 157, 159, 161-163, 167-168, 170-171,
175
actual 39, 47, 138-139, 151, 167, 187, 244, 257
actually 28, 69, 73, 99, 183, 189, 205, 240
addition 110, 189
additional 34, 37, 67, 178, 250

additions   96
address   20, 74, 132, 136
addressed   134, 163, 228, 246
addressing   37
adequate   135, 137, 199, 201, 205, 209, 229, 252
adequately   34, 132, 171, 183, 224
Adjust 90-91
adjusted   95, 222
admissible   250
adopters   193
advance   227-228
advantage   69, 183
advantages   122, 140, 159, 255
adverse   187
affect 63, 66-67, 115, 121, 142, 168, 197, 214, 219
affected   130, 191, 194, 203, 209, 211, 238
affecting   11, 21, 70
affects 167
affordable   74
against39, 90, 144, 150, 224
agencies   130
agenda   132, 227
agendas   120
agents 186
aggregate   47
agreed   192, 209
Agreement   5, 102, 227
agreements   63, 73, 210, 241, 243
agrees 117, 185
aiming 109
alerts   93
aligned   16
Alignment   174
aligns 209
alleged   1
alliance   74
allocate   100
allocated   51, 112, 175
allowable   54
allows 9, 161, 171
almost 240
already   123, 182, 215, 223, 255
altogether   201

always 9, 175
ambitious   229
Amongst   197
amount   24, 239
amplify66, 113
analysis   2, 5, 9-10, 59, 63, 67-68, 80, 130, 135, 138, 154,
167, 173, 177, 179-180, 183, 189, 195, 201, 203, 207-208, 230, 238
analytical   242
analyze   2, 57, 71, 200
analyzed   93, 138, 174
annual 151
another   148, 158, 236
anothers   229
answer 10-11, 15, 27, 43, 57, 73, 88, 100, 182
answered   25, 42, 56, 71, 87, 99, 123
answering   10, 159, 245
anyone   33, 112, 117
anything   163, 183, 222
appear   1
applicable   10, 141, 150, 171, 242, 244
applied   86, 98, 157, 238
appointed   29, 32
approach   77-78, 115, 122, 191, 216, 229-231
approaches   81, 181, 233
approval   108, 251
approvals   139, 153, 192
approve   139, 144
approved   35, 62, 142, 145, 173, 179, 181-182, 184, 219
approvers   139
approving   142, 182, 217
Architects   7
archived   168
archives   253
arising 125
around109, 120, 212
articulate   231
ascertain   150
asking 1, 7, 185
aspects   159, 208, 236
aspiration   236
assertions   243
assess 16, 35, 75, 88, 104, 161
assessed   85, 191

assessing   78, 92
assessment   4-5, 8-9, 17, 139, 173, 197, 199, 206, 208, 229, 231, 243, 257
assets 53, 248
assign 19
assigned   35, 40, 134, 151, 157, 205, 210, 226, 233, 238
assigning   165
assignment   4, 157, 187, 227
assist 8, 68, 89, 177, 187, 221
assistant   7
associated   224
Assuming   199
Assumption   3, 146
assurance   16, 190-191, 205, 221, 252
assure 224
attached   170
attainable   36, 189
attempted   33
attempting   96
attend 25, 207
attendance   29
attended   29
attention   11, 104, 201
attitude   253
attitudes   216
attribute   146
attributes   3, 102, 140, 157, 217
audience   211
audited   174, 253
auditing   18, 92, 101, 238
auditor 242-243
auditors   243
audits 242
author 1
authority   68, 139, 194, 251
authorize   218
authorized   134, 136, 151, 238, 253
automated   153
automatic   254
available   16, 25, 30, 35, 47, 66, 68, 82, 89, 114, 150, 155-156, 158, 181, 188, 195-196, 200-201, 212, 242, 251, 258
Average   11, 25, 42, 56, 71, 87, 99, 123, 167, 169, 245
averse 196

avoided   201
awardee   207
background   9, 224
backing   131
backward   220
balance   189
balanced   79
bandwidth   245
barriers 106, 127
baseline   4, 119, 135, 144, 150, 174, 179
baselined   153, 205
baselines   35, 41
basically   176
basics 111
because   172
become   101, 117, 122-123, 142, 221
becomes   195, 222
before 9, 33, 99, 128, 155, 161-162, 170, 174, 179, 196
beginning   2, 14, 26, 42, 56, 72, 87, 99, 123
begins 221
behavior   237, 253
behaviors   22, 190, 221, 237
behaviour   229, 251
behind 228
belief   10, 15, 27, 43, 57, 73, 88, 100, 104
believable   107
believe 104, 117
Benchmark   184
benefit 1, 15, 18-19, 48, 95, 154
benefits   19, 52, 54-55, 58, 100, 107, 113, 116-118, 135, 146,
234
better 7, 40, 52, 84, 155, 170, 178, 183, 203, 222, 228, 247
between   142, 166, 187, 192-193, 209, 217, 238
beyond   233
bidding   175
biggest   43, 83, 175, 213, 248
bother 43
bottleneck   155
bounce   65, 71
boundaries   34, 137
bounds   34
Breakdown   3, 148, 165
briefed 32, 211

briefly   258
brings   30
broader   236
broken 69
brought   144, 257
budget   90, 98, 114, 134, 136, 150, 153, 155, 170, 172, 180, 198, 242, 244, 247-248, 251
budgeted   47, 188
budgets   19, 107, 151, 238, 248
building   16, 97, 240-241
business   1, 7, 9, 21, 31, 35, 46-48, 59, 61, 80, 93, 105, 108-109, 111, 113, 117, 121, 123, 128, 140, 174, 187, 195, 200, 209, 211, 220, 238, 242-243, 246
busywork   214
buy-in 111
calculate   161, 183
calculated   188
cancelled   251
cannot162, 171
capability   16, 180, 224
capable   7, 38
capacities   117, 133
capacity   16, 81, 132, 176, 234, 237
capitalize   71, 230
capture   95, 146, 208, 254
captured   46, 58, 82, 117, 191, 205-206, 209, 218
career 142
careers   108
carefully   202
carried 62, 203, 257
carrying   218
cash-drain   130
Cashflow   130
categories   238
category   33
caught230
caused   1, 53
causes 49, 51, 53-54, 57-58, 67, 70, 89, 132, 203, 238
causing   21
celebrate   85, 225
celebrated   236
center 51, 134
centrally   79

certain 193
Certified   210
challenge   7, 222, 257
challenges   111, 159
champion   34
chance   203
chances   195
change   5, 15, 25, 40, 44, 48, 59 60, 68-69, 71, 75, 77, 83-84, 96, 116, 129, 138-139, 144, 148, 162, 171, 173, 175-176, 179, 186, 199, 211-212, 217-220, 233, 239, 253
changed   25, 40, 77, 92, 107, 125, 140, 177, 179, 212
changes   23, 32, 34-35, 50, 62, 74, 86, 96, 99, 107, 114, 118, 134, 136, 144, 147, 150-151, 165, 172-173, 179, 181, 201, 209, 217-219, 225, 231, 253, 256-257
changing   90, 120
channels   140
chargeable   238
charged   45
charter 2, 28, 40, 86, 127-128, 134
charters   31
charts 58, 171
cheaper   52
checked   71, 89, 95, 97
Checking   181
checklists   8, 191
choice 33, 111, 228
choose   10, 74
chosen 199, 213, 234
circumvent   21
claimed   1
claims 251
clarify 109
clarity 145
classes 137
classified   151
clearly 10, 15, 19, 27, 37-38, 41, 43, 57, 73, 82, 88, 100, 174, 190, 209, 229
client   44, 116, 213, 246, 255
clients 22, 33, 234
closed 97, 150, 174, 219, 253
closely 9
Close-Out   6, 205, 253-256
closest 110

Closing 6, 248
Coaches   39-40
coding 147
cognitive   237
cognizant   236
colleague   109
colleagues   100-101, 169
collect 63, 90, 177
collected   32, 40, 57-60, 62, 224
collection   63
coming   67, 207
command   92
comments   208, 246
commit   230
commitment   92, 117, 132, 185, 202, 239
committed   69, 136, 191, 196, 242
committee   137, 147
common   145, 168, 174-175, 193
community   139, 169, 177-178, 197, 203
companies   1, 89, 222
company   7, 52, 69, 104-105, 109, 113, 117, 123
compare   68, 181, 240
compared   108, 167
comparing   81
comparison   10
compatible   220
compelling   28
competing   51, 251
competitor   239
compile   182
complains   229
complaint   230
complaints   197, 224
complete   1, 8, 10, 21, 33, 39-40, 135, 157, 166, 168, 192,
196, 201, 228, 242, 246, 253
completed   11, 28, 32, 36, 38, 128, 161-162, 206, 225, 253
completely   105, 169
completing   148, 162
completion   28, 30, 150, 161-162, 180, 225, 237, 239-240
complex   7, 240
complexity   18, 51, 70, 217
compliance   18, 52, 67, 73, 127, 210
complied   225

comply	242, 250
components	168, 191, 209
compute	11
computing	105
concept	78, 145, 185
concern	55, 74
concerned	24
concerns	22, 110, 244
concrete	86, 229
condition	94, 171
conditions	97, 122, 131, 135, 199, 242
conducted	173, 179, 207, 210, 232
confidence	161, 183, 196
confirm	10
conflict138	
conflicts	213, 225
conform	146
confronted	195
conjure	140-141
connected	172
connecting	109
consensus	255
consider	21-22, 168, 176, 207, 228
considered	16, 22, 45, 242
considers	69, 182
consistent	29, 45, 59, 94, 150, 188, 237, 239
constitute	236
Constraint	3, 146, 242
consultant	7, 176
consulted	105
consulting	55
consumers	107
contact	7, 173, 181
contacts	122, 211
contain	22, 63, 97
contained	1, 150
contains	8
content	37, 135, 201
contents	1-2, 8, 233
context	33, 36
continual	88, 97
continuity	46
continuous	63, 86

contract   6, 136, 151, 175, 187-188, 207-208, 210, 215, 225, 239, 251, 253-254
contractor   5, 151, 167, 238, 244, 252
contracts   63, 159, 168, 243-244, 252-253
contribute   133, 140
control 2, 29, 54, 59, 88, 90, 92-94, 96, 98, 131, 138-139, 144, 150, 168, 172, 178, 187, 217-218, 221, 238
controlled   59
controls   22, 61, 68, 74-75, 77, 92, 94-95, 98-99, 197-198, 203, 252
convention   110
convey   1, 136
cooperate   178
copies 251
Copyright   1
corporate   223
correct43, 88
corrected   174
correction   151
corrective   89, 150
correctly   132, 224
correspond   8-9
cosmetic   147
costing47
counting   155
course 40, 48, 240
covering   8, 90, 189
covers 242
coworker   116
craziest   117
create 22, 111, 113, 122, 144, 182, 184, 243
created   65-66, 91, 129, 133-135, 137, 154, 197, 204, 213
creating   7, 43
creative   25
creativity   85
credible   178
criteria 2, 4, 8-9, 33, 36-37, 60, 75, 92, 113, 124, 134, 142, 144, 173, 177, 207, 253
CRITERION   2, 15, 27, 43, 57, 73, 88, 100
critical 36-37, 40, 66, 76, 89, 92, 123, 155, 159, 167, 213-214, 222, 232, 248
criticism   65
crucial 62, 131, 159, 167

crystal 10
culture 33, 70, 132, 183, 202, 210-211
current 30, 43, 46, 65-66, 68, 77, 85, 98, 101, 104, 107, 122, 147, 150, 168, 182, 186, 188, 197, 202, 214, 217, 248
currently   29, 101, 188
custom 21
customer   23, 29, 31-32, 36, 40-41, 77, 90, 95, 105, 107, 109, 114, 118, 140, 181-182, 196, 200, 202
customers   1, 24, 30, 38, 52-53, 67-68, 96, 102, 106, 108, 114, 116-120, 122, 130, 146, 181, 191, 199, 203, 216, 225
cut-down   240
damage   1, 202
Dashboard   8
dashboards   96
day-to-day   88, 109, 159
deadlines   16, 116, 159
dealing   18
deceitful   116
decide 76, 168
decided   74, 225
deciding   115
decision   5, 52, 66, 76-77, 83-84, 207, 221
decisions   74-75, 78-80, 86, 91, 94, 97, 128, 191, 205, 222, 225-226, 232
decomposed 167
dedicated   7
deeper   10, 236
defect 137, 183
defects   183
define 2, 27, 30, 33, 60, 66, 138, 145, 169, 176, 200, 221, 237
defined   10, 15, 17, 22, 27, 31-32, 34-41, 43, 57, 59, 65, 73, 88, 100, 144-145, 147, 157, 179, 184, 190, 205, 209
defines 24, 32, 36, 165
defining   7, 123, 127
definite   97, 157
definition   19, 23, 35, 37, 39, 147, 154, 173
degree   196, 229-232, 236-237
delaying   55
delays 171
delegated   38
delete 175
deletions   96
deliver 24, 36, 77, 108, 117, 178

delivered   46, 113, 166, 171, 179, 205, 225, 235, 249
deliveries   250
delivering   136
delivery   17, 122, 133, 209, 253
demand   121, 195, 200
demands   230
department   7, 113, 216
depend   215
dependent   128, 248
depends   104
depict 161
deploy 93, 119, 223
deployed   93, 139
deploying   55
deployment   47
derive 92
describe   138, 142, 146, 176, 244
described   1, 219
describes   167
describing   38
deserving   215
design 1, 9, 61, 69, 82, 92, 115, 132, 181, 195, 201, 251
designated   207
designed   7, 9, 67, 84
designing   7
desired22, 34, 60, 85, 165, 220, 240, 258
detail   144-145, 148, 154, 157, 170, 201, 255
detailed   66, 136, 146, 156, 192, 231
details 212
detect 97
determine   9, 116, 121, 155, 167, 177, 182
determined   66, 121, 185, 251
detracting   101
develop   51, 73, 80-83, 134, 139, 148, 176, 230
developed   9, 28, 31, 38, 48, 86, 138, 146, 186, 211, 220, 235,
240-241
developers   202
developing   71, 81, 212
develops   231
deviation   168, 233
device 224
devices   224, 228
diagnostic   203

diagram   3, 49, 52, 70, 161-162, 171
diagrams   43
dictates   172
Dictionary   3, 150
differ   171
difference   126, 166
different   7, 18, 27-28, 30, 41, 68, 70, 105, 121, 133, 189,
199, 209, 222, 255
difficult 62, 156-157, 161, 165, 175
difficulty   214
dilemma   107
dimensions   17
direct   150-151, 238-239
direction   40, 52
directions   203
directly 1, 67-68, 255
directors   242
Directory   5, 225
Disagree   10, 15, 27, 43, 57, 73, 88, 100
disaster   46, 51
disclosure   89
discover   139
discussion   122
displayed   40, 71, 155, 170
disputes   253
disqualify   69
disruptive   59
distribute   225
Divided   25, 38, 42, 56, 71, 86, 99, 123
document   9, 41, 128, 174, 221
documented 39, 76, 82, 89, 91, 95, 98, 144, 146, 154, 179, 181,
189-190, 218, 238, 246, 250
documents   7, 168, 209, 251
dollar   239
dollars 239
domains   82
dormant   122
drawing   199
Driver   67
drivers 55, 61, 211
drives   50
driving 100
dropped   153

duplicate   182
duplicates   138
duration   3, 148, 167-169, 205, 242
durations   39, 153-154, 213
during 40, 78, 125-126, 137, 163, 183, 191, 195, 199, 203, 207, 257
duties 187, 218, 231
dynamics   36
earliest 138
earned   5, 240
easily   144, 236
economic   203
economical   106
economy   85, 168
eDiscovery   221-222
edition 8
editorial   1
educate   249, 255
education   19, 98, 130, 224, 243
effect 223
effective   23-24, 103, 110, 121, 141, 150, 154, 169, 203, 221, 223-224, 231, 243, 252, 257
effects 50, 131, 159-160, 225
efficiency   59, 96
efficient   78, 191, 215, 252
effort   38, 47, 49-50, 103, 134, 137, 151, 191, 233
efforts 33, 248
electronic   1
element   151
elements   9, 31, 60, 89, 121, 144-145, 150, 167, 186-187, 226, 238
e-mail 140
embarking   28
embrace   211
emergency   243
emerging   95
emphasis   221
employed   209
employee   76, 102, 244
employees   16, 22, 24, 61, 101, 106, 116, 176, 181
employers   129
employment   242
empower   7

enable 59
enablers   109
encourage   85, 93, 230
encouraged   188
end-users   200
engage   110, 194, 227, 230
engagement   129, 193, 197, 206, 227
enhance   91, 230
enhanced   108
enhancing   91
enlarged   199
enough   7, 62, 104, 122, 139, 142, 242
ensure 39, 64, 69, 103-104, 114-115, 120, 127, 168, 181, 185, 208-209, 213, 225, 228
ensures   115
ensuring   9, 112, 240-241
Enterprise   67, 215
entire   187
entities 48, 135, 223
entity   1, 140, 231
envisaged   133
equipment   17, 251
equipped   30
equitably   38
errors   103, 147, 151, 175
escalated   206
Escalation   173
essence   128, 136, 230
essential   85
essentials   111
establish   73, 93, 178
estimate   45, 48, 51, 134-135, 168, 170, 196, 246
estimated   28, 30, 45, 50, 103, 173, 177, 196, 198, 244
estimates   3-4, 30, 45, 61, 134, 146, 150, 167, 175, 239
estimating   3-4, 136, 153, 169, 177, 192
estimation   80, 132, 168, 192, 209, 258
estimator   176
etcetera   51, 122
ethical 17, 109, 234
ethics   200
ethnic   113
European   250
evaluate   74, 79-80, 131, 144, 201

evaluated 224
evaluation 60, 81, 89, 134, 208, 234
events 25, 80, 83, 86
everyday 61
everyone 29, 38, 145, 185, 223, 227
everything 52, 222
evidence 10, 51, 130, 184, 197, 216, 243, 251
evolution 43
evolve 94
exactly 223
examine 243
examined 33
examining 224
example 2, 8, 12, 17, 64, 93, 137, 151, 230
examples 7-8, 128
exceed 148
excellence 7
excellent 43
except 151
excessive 201
exclude 74
excluded 150
executed 179, 219
Executing 5, 210, 213
execution 93, 167, 217
executive 7, 107, 192
executives 123
exercise 22
exercises 229
existence 204
existing 9, 93, 102, 127, 135, 239
expect 119, 180
expected 19, 39, 77, 120, 125, 167-168, 176, 181, 222, 234, 256
expend 50
expense 238
experience 39, 110, 115, 119, 169, 176, 190, 223-224, 238, 244
experiment 120
expertise 134, 192, 227
experts 41
explained 9
explicitly 112
explore 70, 231

explored   182, 200
exposure   197
exposures   74
express 130
expressed   134
extent 10, 18, 24, 38, 81, 133, 187, 242-243
external   33, 113
facilitate   10, 17, 70, 96, 237
facing 21, 107, 198
factors 49, 78, 101, 177, 201, 214
failed   51
failure 46, 113, 116, 224
fairly   38
falling   153
familiar 8
families 176
fashion 1, 35
feasible   48, 69, 113, 178
feature 9
features   246
feedback   31-32, 51, 190, 228
Filter   183
finalize 205
finalized   12
financial   52, 58, 61, 71, 106, 108, 131, 151, 234
fingertips   9
finish   127, 138, 155-157, 240-241
finished   127
fixing   258
follow   89, 103, 110, 246
followed   30, 136, 147, 250, 257
following   8, 10, 185, 251
follow-up   133
forecast   240
forecasts   150
forefront   120
foresee   159
foreseen   125
forever 107
forget 9
formal 6, 174, 199, 209, 237, 246-247, 257
formally   34, 171, 196
format 9

formed40, 232
formula   11, 110
Formulate   27
formulated   135, 227
forward   104
forwarded   187
foster   102, 113
framework   92, 105, 185-186
freaky 122
frequency   37, 92, 101, 258
frequent   145
frequently   45, 231, 236
friend   103, 107, 109
friends 176
frontiers   77
fulfill   103
full-blown   47
full-scale   82
fulltime 136
function   145, 234, 246, 251
functional   150
functions   58, 114-115, 190, 226
funded154
funding   115, 122, 146, 248
further 197
future   7, 52, 93-94, 122, 135, 199-200
gained96-97
gather 10, 28, 32, 36, 38, 40-41, 43, 58, 62, 182
gathered   35, 61-62, 65-67, 138
gathering   31, 41, 140
general   75, 157, 223, 246, 251
generally   215, 239
generate   67
generated   126, 239
generation   8, 60
geographic   130
getting50, 221
global 85, 105, 130
govern103
governance   22, 102, 190, 231
granted   180
graphical   171
graphics   18

graphs 8
greatest 75, 257
ground 58
groups 121, 146, 165, 191, 209, 216
growth 101, 257
guarantee 83
guaranteed 32
guidance 1
guidelines 134, 221
handle 164, 225
handled 208
happen 23, 114, 197, 203-204, 223
happening 105, 130
happens 7, 35, 49, 55, 101-102, 122, 136, 177, 183, 203-204, 253
hardest 45
hardly 240
hardware 213, 258
havent 104
having 137, 224
hazards 203-204
health 112, 224
hearing 113
helping 7, 145, 213
hidden 50
higher 151, 183
highest 16
high-level 32, 36, 140
highlight 189
Highly 70
high-tech 101
hijacking 108
hinder 131, 147
hiring 96
Historical 177, 238
history 155
hitters 58
hitting 241
honest 109
horizon 110
humans 7
hypotheses 57

identified   1, 16, 19-20, 23, 36, 41, 68, 75, 86, 125, 136, 145, 150-152, 174, 179, 183, 189, 191-192, 197, 199, 202, 205, 208, 221, 238, 248
identify9-10, 23-24, 64, 74, 144, 150, 167, 177, 187, 239
identity229
ignore 20
ignoring   123
images140-141
imbedded   97
immediate   198
impact4, 27, 43, 46-49, 51-52, 82, 120, 126, 130, 140, 168, 173, 179, 197, 199, 201, 219, 230-231, 233-234, 257-258
impacted   44, 146-147
impacts   45, 53, 133, 146-147, 169, 218
implement   16, 50, 69, 88
importance   236
important   20, 23, 29, 62, 67-68, 114, 118-119, 121, 125, 132-133, 165, 180, 183, 193, 233
improve   2, 9, 60, 73, 75-81, 84-86, 125, 183, 248-249, 255-257
improved   76, 84-85, 97
improves   126
improving   74, 216
inactive   175
incentives   96
incident   197
include   21, 74, 172-173, 209
included   2, 7, 52, 132, 169, 175, 178, 188, 218, 244, 253
INCLUDES   9
including   16, 29, 39-40, 52, 55, 59, 89-90, 97, 151
increase   81, 109, 239
increased   106, 189
increasing   107, 221
incurred   48
indemnity   242
in-depth   8, 10
indicate   69, 94, 113, 188
indicated   89
indicators   20, 49, 54, 59, 65-66, 68, 85, 97, 182, 201
indirect   45, 151, 175, 187
indirectly   1
individual   1, 47, 156, 205, 236, 244, 255
industry   92, 108-109, 168

infinite 105
influence   77, 121, 129, 205, 221, 255
influenced   243
influences   130, 193
informal   236-237
informed   118
ingrained   95
inherent   104
initial   40, 115, 182
initially 39
initiate 150
initiated   178, 219
Initiating   2, 114, 125
initiative   10, 186, 211
Innovate   73
innovation   54, 59, 66, 85, 89, 113, 115
innovative   122, 133, 177
in-process   59
inputs   27, 38, 53, 68, 99, 126
inside   24
insight 66-67
insights 8
inspection   197
inspired   110
Instead122
instructed   138-139
insurance   242
insure   104
integrate   77, 90, 111, 134
integrated   208
integrity   16, 123, 219
intended   1, 79
INTENT 15, 27, 43, 57, 73, 88, 100, 223
intention   1
intentions   223-224
interact   114
interest104, 183, 216
interested   235
interests   24, 211, 256
intergroup   229
interim 116
internal   1, 33, 63, 111, 113, 136, 151, 154, 159, 187, 197,
209

interpret   10
intervals   136, 154, 192
interview   118, 255
introduce   197
introduced   231
inventory   151, 175
invest 62
investment   24, 44, 185-186
investor   53
invoices   174
involve 103, 131
involved   24, 32, 58, 64-65, 81, 108, 131, 133, 136, 139-140, 146, 187, 191-192, 212, 216, 234, 250-251, 254, 257
involves   92
involving   224
issues   16, 18, 20, 22-23, 141, 153, 161, 163, 188, 191, 206, 209, 213, 228, 238, 256, 258
itself   1, 22
jointly 229
judgment   1
justify 197
killer   122
knowledge   9, 29, 33, 39, 75, 91, 95-98, 102, 118-119, 189-190, 211, 232, 253
labeled   187
labeling   224
labour 252
lacked 91
lacking 201
languages   227
laptops   228
largely 65
latest   8
laundry   138
leader 23, 34, 70-71, 85, 195
leaders 29, 40, 65, 92, 114, 119, 182, 193
leadership   22, 30, 39, 85, 112, 119, 132
learned   6, 95, 117, 185, 247, 255, 257
learning   89, 91, 95, 221
lesson   255
lessons 6, 82, 95, 117, 185, 247, 255, 257
letter   140

levels   16, 66, 68, 85, 91, 94, 112, 148, 151, 182, 185, 203, 238, 242
leverage   37, 85, 95, 110, 177, 227
leveraged   33
levers 212
liability 1, 242
licensed   1
lifecycle   55, 61, 199
Lifetime   9
likelihood   79, 86, 197
likely   81, 98, 109, 179, 199-200, 207, 222
limitation   46
limited 9
linked 34, 141
linking 243
listed   1, 186
listen   101, 106, 228
little   138
locally 79, 251
locations   181
logged217
logical 163
logically   154
longer 92
long-term   90, 106, 120
losing 53
losses   41
lowest 150
machines   213
magnitude   81
maintain   88, 101, 123, 181
maintained   83, 151, 187, 250
makers84, 99
making   23, 66, 74, 77, 114, 185, 213
manage   32-33, 39, 44, 49, 52, 60, 69, 77, 82-84, 102, 118, 137, 139, 142, 145, 147, 159, 172, 192-195, 211, 226, 229
manageable 31, 80, 168, 191
managed   7, 41, 58, 64, 68, 76, 79-80, 83, 95-96, 138, 200, 205, 217, 246, 251

management 1, 3-5, 8-9, 15, 23-24, 39-40, 54, 60, 64, 66-67, 69, 71, 76-79, 81, 83, 86, 110-111, 118, 121, 125, 130-131, 133-136, 138, 145, 147, 150, 153-154, 157, 168, 171, 173-174, 179, 181, 185-187, 191-193, 195, 199, 205-207, 209, 211-212, 214, 216, 223, 226, 234-235, 238, 240, 243, 246-247, 254

manager   7, 9, 25, 28, 39, 119, 136, 167, 205, 210, 216
managers   2, 124, 150, 196
manages   79, 83, 127, 244
managing   2, 76, 124, 129, 168, 256
mandatory   219
manner   78, 150, 188, 191, 230, 239
mantle 122
mapped   30
Mapping   62, 64-65
margin 154, 238
market 15, 168, 202, 240
marketer   7
marketing   107, 140
markets   17
material   151, 181, 183, 238-239, 252
materials   1, 227-228, 251
matrices   142
Matrix 2-4, 130, 142, 187, 201
matter 41, 49, 54
mature 139
meaning   228
meaningful   49, 109, 151, 195
measurable   29, 36, 224
measure   2, 9, 18, 37, 40, 43-45, 47, 50-52, 54-55, 59, 67, 73, 79, 82-83, 91, 96, 98, 130, 133, 144, 177, 183, 201, 214
measured   21, 46, 48, 50-51, 53, 55, 85, 90, 99, 151, 181, 229, 236
measures   45, 47, 50, 52, 54, 59-60, 66, 68, 85, 91, 94, 97, 133, 182, 203, 217-218, 230, 257
measuring   91
mechanical   1
mechanism   146
mechanisms   130, 133, 185
medium   240
meeting   28, 41, 95, 185, 209, 216, 222, 225, 227-228, 255
meetings   29, 31-32, 34, 136, 154, 221, 228
megatrends   121
member   5, 39, 105, 112, 193, 215, 228, 231, 243

members   32, 35, 37-39, 41, 63, 89, 136, 138, 153, 192-193, 205, 218, 225-231, 236-237, 251
membership   229
mental 243
message   91
messages   233, 255
method   53, 132, 157, 168-169, 182, 229
methods   31, 37, 48, 58, 177, 195, 200, 209, 252
metrics 4, 31, 60, 96, 139, 180, 183-184, 195
Milestone   3, 159, 173
milestones   40, 129, 150, 157, 162, 173, 251
minimal   229
minimize   126, 172, 234
minimizing   64
minimum   242, 245
minority   24
minutes   41, 76, 209, 225
missed 47, 113
missing 68, 101, 157-158, 188
mission 67, 69, 119, 121
Mitigate   76, 126
mitigated   248
mitigating   192
mitigation   136
mobile 228
mobilized   133
modeling   65, 181, 186
models 16, 52, 66, 117, 243
modern   192, 242
modified   93
moment   108
moments   62
momentum   113-114
monetary   15
monitor   89, 91, 93-94, 96, 130, 153, 177, 251
monitored   93, 96-97, 125, 155, 167, 170, 191
monitoring   5, 88, 91, 94-96, 164, 201, 217, 234, 239
monthly   238
months 76, 83
motivate   104, 237
motivation   19, 97
motive 185
moving   104

multiple   139, 196, 209, 238
narrative   159
narrow 58
national   133, 203
native 227
nature 151
nearest   11
nearly 117
necessary   59, 64, 66, 69, 117-118, 122, 132, 177, 192, 195,
213, 219, 223-224, 237, 250, 258
needed   16-21, 23, 27, 57, 68-69, 94, 97-99, 140, 174, 177,
207
negative   100
negatively   214
negotiate   116
negotiated   102
neither 1
network   3, 161-162, 167, 171, 236
Neutral 10, 15, 27, 43, 57, 73, 88, 100
normal 95
normalized   207
Notice 1
noticing   222
notified   254
notify 227
number   25, 42, 50, 56, 71, 86, 99, 123, 157, 165, 182-183,
199, 201, 259
numbers   115
numerous   253
objection   15, 20
objective   7, 50, 125, 133, 144
objectives   16, 23, 25, 27, 34, 39, 67, 69, 90, 92, 108, 113, 118,
121, 134, 140, 146, 171, 173-174, 193, 204, 209, 216, 226, 258
observe   190
observed   74
obsolete   121
obstacles   21, 159, 177
obstruct   131
obtain 106, 167, 247
obtained   32, 192
obtaining   53
obvious   230
obviously   10

occurred   182
occurring   80, 125, 197
occurs 51, 99, 132
offerings   68
offers   207
office   207, 216, 254
officers 208, 242
officials 253
offshore   141
onboarding   154
one-time   7
ongoing   99, 155, 170
on-going   153
opened   150
opening   250
operate   203
operates   109
operating   5, 43, 47, 94, 133, 217, 227
operation   94, 169, 179
operations   9, 90-91, 95-96, 179, 224
operators   89, 183
opponent   222
opponents   233
opposed   233
opposite   104, 109
opposition   107
optimal   78, 207, 245
optimize   77, 91
optimized   107
optimiztic   168
option 111, 231
options 25
orders   175, 210
organized   250
orient   95
oriented   191, 258
original 153, 172, 191, 206
originate   99, 194
others   138, 172, 178, 181-182, 189, 198, 222, 230, 237, 249, 255
otherwise   1
outcome   10, 83, 165, 251
outcomes   78, 91, 103, 130, 178, 235, 240, 255, 257-258
outlined   92

output 37, 60, 63-64, 66-67, 69-70, 94, 97
outputs   38, 58-61, 68, 70, 99, 163, 209
outside85, 250
outsource   65, 168, 254
outweigh   55
overall 9-10, 16, 54, 90, 112, 121, 125, 132, 140, 161, 171, 183,
197, 221, 223, 234, 244
overcome   177
overhead   151, 188, 238
overlook   193
overlooked   248
oversees   126
oversight   63, 147
overtime   157
ownership   38, 98
package   238
packages   151
packaging   224
paradigms   107
paragraph   101
parallel   161
parameters   89, 181
Pareto 58
particular   64
Parties 74, 135, 253-254
partners   24, 32, 74, 95, 104, 116, 119, 133, 159, 234
pattern   157
patterns   81
paycheck   117
paying 104
payment   153, 174, 251, 253
payments   136, 251
pending   219
people7, 19, 43, 48, 65, 68, 81, 83, 91, 93, 101, 106, 108, 110,
112, 114, 120-122, 187-188, 196, 199-201, 203, 210, 212, 215, 240,
242
perceive   112
percentage   142
perception   79, 109
perform   19, 35, 37-38, 138, 155, 167, 217
performed   142, 155-156, 187-188, 208, 224, 226
performing   125, 198, 207, 223
perhaps   25, 240

period 84, 188
periods 151
permission   1
permitting   182
person 1
personal   121, 258
personally   142, 258
personnel   15, 20, 63, 93, 162, 171, 186, 192, 224
pertinent   93
phases 55, 75, 157, 195, 255
Philosophy   130
pitfalls 104
places 208
planet 91
planned   92, 94-95, 138-139, 163, 167, 169, 187-188, 198,
209, 255-256
planners   99
planning   3, 8, 89, 99, 126, 132, 134, 138, 146, 161, 163, 215,
223, 238
plates 250
players 82
please 207
pocket 178
pockets   178
points 25, 42, 56, 70-71, 86, 99, 123
poking 168
policies   130, 134, 212, 251
policy 39, 79, 99, 127, 147, 163, 223, 250-251
Political   112, 160
portfolio   122, 234, 251
portion 251
portray 58
position   242
positioned   177-178
positions   242
positive   83, 100, 113, 229
possess 229
possible   49, 51, 58, 67, 80, 88, 105, 111, 137, 168-169, 187,
224, 237
potential   22, 49, 69, 80, 86, 111, 120-121, 140, 187, 202, 231
practical   69, 73, 76, 88, 215-216
practices   1, 9, 64, 81, 95-96, 192, 211, 246, 250
precaution   1

precludes   207
predict 127, 217
predicting   91
Prediction   198
predictor   165
pre-filled   8
prepare   185, 189, 227, 257
preparing   172, 255
present   94, 115, 122, 232, 250
presented   19, 250
preserve   29
preserved   70
pressures   159
prevent   55, 130, 147, 174, 214
preventive   203
prevents   23
previous   33, 171, 183, 244
previously   134, 219
priced 151
primary   53, 165, 167
principles   134, 192
priorities   44, 46-47, 51, 54, 211
prioritize   199, 242
priority 50-51
privacy   32
private 133
problem   15-19, 21, 23, 25, 27, 33, 36, 38, 40, 46-47, 69, 136,
140, 167, 215, 222, 240
problems   17-18, 20-22, 80, 83, 89, 115, 132, 140, 186, 257
procedure   227, 250
procedures   9, 76, 89, 91, 94, 98, 136-137, 147, 163, 175, 179,
182, 185, 209, 212, 221, 238, 242, 250
proceeding   170, 191
process   1-7, 9, 27-28, 30, 33, 36-38, 46, 57, 59-71, 74, 88,
93-98, 125, 127, 132, 137-140, 142-144, 146-147, 153-154, 163,
169, 172, 174, 181, 185-186, 199, 202, 207, 210, 213, 222, 225-226,
231, 234, 240-244, 246, 248, 250-251, 256
processes   30, 46, 54, 58-60, 63, 65-67, 69-71, 89, 93, 96, 126,
144, 147, 181-182, 186, 209, 211, 213, 220, 224, 234, 246, 250
produce   68, 126-127, 133, 163, 215, 234
produced   70, 83, 144, 234, 257
produces   157
producing   142

288

product   1, 45, 66, 68, 120, 122, 139, 179, 182-184, 201, 215-216, 219, 225, 240-242, 246, 249, 255, 257
production   40, 106, 147
productive   187
products   1, 17, 20, 43, 102, 115, 127, 133, 142, 151, 183, 214, 216, 220, 229, 250
program   45, 67, 90, 126, 132-133, 181, 189, 197, 234-235, 243
programme   213, 234
programs   133-134, 168, 215
progress   32, 53, 79, 90, 106, 114, 133, 144, 150, 153, 177, 182, 185, 205, 213-214, 224, 228, 235, 251
prohibited   151
project 2-8, 19, 21, 28, 47, 58, 61, 64, 78, 92, 95, 99, 103, 112-115, 119, 121, 124-125, 127-142, 144-148, 150-151, 153-157, 159, 161-162, 165, 167-175, 177-180, 188-189, 191-192, 194-202, 205-206, 209-211, 213-216, 219-220, 226, 230, 233-236, 240, 244, 246-251, 253, 255-258
projected   150-151
projects   2, 54, 119, 124, 126, 128, 130, 133, 135, 137, 142, 145, 147, 168, 171, 196-197, 209, 215-216, 225, 240-241, 248, 257
promising   122
promote   43, 65, 243
promotion   189
promptly   206
proofing   74
proper 89, 139, 153, 187
properly   29, 125, 151
proponents   233
proposal   159
proposals   99, 167, 208
proposed   16, 50-51, 130, 134, 140, 211, 244-245, 248
Propriety   234
protect   61, 111
protected   70
proved 246
provide   66, 103, 106, 108, 129, 135, 150, 175, 177, 214, 230, 236, 238
provided   11, 89, 191
provider   211
providers   74
providing   89, 129, 144, 159
provision   154, 191

public 132-133, 206, 242
publisher   1
purchase   7, 207, 210, 225
purchased   151
purchases   252
purchasing   250
purpose   2, 9, 119, 128, 165, 172, 177, 185, 218, 222, 231, 236-237
pushing   122
qualified   38, 62-64, 70, 174
qualifies   60, 71
qualify 53, 62
quality 1, 4-5, 9, 16, 50-51, 54, 63, 68, 70-71, 77, 91, 98, 109, 131, 133, 153, 168, 181, 183-186, 190-191, 201, 205, 210, 221, 223
quantified   94
quantify   53
question   10, 15, 27, 43, 57, 73, 88, 100, 114, 227
questions   7-8, 10, 69, 193
quickly 9, 64-65, 71, 195
radically   59
raised 191
ranking217
rather 118
rational   239
rationale   174, 221
reached   25
reaching   121
reactivate   122
reader 136
readiness   40, 173
readings   89
realism 207
realistic   25, 64, 116, 134, 154, 172, 200-201, 236
reality 195, 223
realize 56
realized   118, 246
really   7, 29
reason 104, 108
reasonable   80, 121, 135-136, 146, 154, 242, 252
reasons   28, 150, 183, 250
reassess   154, 191
re-assign   158
rebuild 122

receive   8-9, 28, 55, 207, 233
received   32, 116, 195, 205, 208, 250, 257
receiving   251
recently   107
recipient   18, 253
recognised   81
recognize   2, 15, 20-22, 24, 81, 85
recognized   16, 18, 20, 22, 24-25, 62, 193, 231
recognizes   25
recommend   107, 109
record 250
recorded   174, 217
recording   1, 227
records   68, 103, 151, 181, 187, 210, 238, 253
recourse   250
recovery   46
redefine   25, 33
re-design   69
reduce 44, 53, 182, 187, 198, 242
reduced   203
reducing   95, 107
references   259
reflect 90, 92, 98, 151, 255
reform 44, 99, 113, 120, 133
reforms 16, 48, 51
regarding   105, 121, 138, 146, 175, 181, 208, 216
Register   2, 4, 129, 138, 197
regret 77
regular 32, 34, 62, 145, 244
regularly   29, 32, 41
regulated   217
regulation   201
regulatory   18, 181
reinforce   181
reinforced   133
reject 139, 144, 211
rejection   250
relate 71, 214, 220
related 15, 55, 65, 99, 126, 182, 190, 217, 240, 255
relating   179
relation   17, 24, 80, 119
relations   113
relative 90, 182, 236

release 139, 147, 183, 255
released   251
releases   244
relevant   36, 48, 66, 92, 102, 146, 180, 190, 238
reliable 30, 203
reliably 229
reluctance   232
remain 37, 223
remaining   177
remember   169
remunerate   76
repair   137, 224
repeat 132
rephrased   9
replace   49, 248
replicate   182
report 5, 76, 89, 153, 184, 197, 205, 215, 236, 244, 251, 255
reported   138, 150, 224, 240
reporting   60, 97, 112, 137, 150, 236
reports 55, 98, 129, 144, 187, 205, 210, 223, 251
repository   174, 210
represent   85, 219-220, 249
reproduced   1
reputation   108
request   5, 69, 173, 179, 217-220
requested   1, 74, 219
requests   207, 217
require 28, 47, 65, 70, 93, 163, 197, 236
required   17, 22, 29, 31, 33, 39-41, 62-63, 74, 91, 125-126,
156-158, 168, 171, 176, 190, 193, 210-211, 213, 223, 228, 243, 255-
256
requiring   129, 253
research   15, 101, 122, 224
reserve 150
reserved   1
reserves   187
reside 86, 174, 207
residual   151
resolution   66, 83
resolve 22-23, 158, 225
resolved   191, 195, 206, 233
resource   3-4, 119, 139, 146, 151, 154, 157-158, 163, 165,
168, 191-192, 215

resources   2, 7, 16-17, 20, 24, 30, 34, 54, 60, 91-93, 100, 105, 112, 119, 133-134, 138, 156 158, 162, 165, 171, 177, 209, 229, 232, 236
respect   1
respected   251
respective   132
respond   187
responded   11
response   16, 89, 93-94, 97, 208, 245
responses   82, 100
responsive   169, 178
restrict 141
result   83, 85, 176, 178, 183, 194, 219, 229, 253, 256
resulted   90
resulting   58
results   8, 36, 39, 68, 73, 76-79, 81, 85-86, 89, 97, 133, 167-168, 171, 177, 181, 191, 213-214, 234, 246
Retain 100
retention   44
return   83, 106, 185-186
revenue   23, 52
revenues   53
review 9, 40, 64, 134, 175, 179, 197, 221, 224
reviewed   38, 171, 183, 192, 224
Reviewer   229, 231
reviews 153, 162, 173, 191, 199, 210
revised 61, 90, 203
revisions   253
revisit   222
reward 43, 47, 63, 215
rewarded   16
rewards   96
rework 49
rights   1
routine 98, 151, 238
routinely   224
rubbish 224
safeguard   130
safety   115, 228
samples   181-182
sampling   181
satisfied   101, 246, 255
satisfies 241

satisfying 110
savings 30, 55-56, 61
scalable 77
scaled 153
scenario 36, 41
schedule 3-4, 29, 98, 139, 150, 153-154, 161-162, 167, 171-174, 179, 187, 191, 197-198, 201, 205, 213, 219, 225, 244, 257
scheduled 137-138, 150
schedules 161, 171-172, 198
scheduling 136, 150, 153, 192, 236, 239
scheme 97
Science 57, 169
scientific 169
scopes 144
Scorecard 2, 11-13
scorecards 96
Scores 13
scoring 9
screen 227
screening 184
seamless 104
second 11
section 11, 25, 42, 56, 71, 86-87, 99, 123
sector 240
securing 109
security 18, 63, 76, 88, 129, 147, 219
segmented 41
segments 30, 121, 238
select 59, 90
selected 75, 134-135, 177, 207, 238
selecting 64, 227
Selection 4, 207
selects 231
seller 208
sellers 1, 167
selling 118, 222, 238
-selling 238
senior 92, 112, 119, 121, 182, 230
sensitive 34, 55
separated 151
sequencing 113, 154, 168
series 10
servers 213

service 1-2, 7, 45, 74, 79, 91, 122, 179, 182, 207, 215-216, 257
services   1, 28, 43, 55, 102 103, 105, 223, 235, 238, 244, 253
session 138
setbacks   65, 71
setting 106, 116
several 68
severely   69
severity   198
shared 96, 177, 238
sharing 67, 75, 91, 227
shifts   25
shortest   168
short-term   236
should 7, 16, 23, 25, 28, 32-33, 35, 43, 49, 55, 57-59, 62, 75, 78-79,
96, 99, 101, 103, 105, 108, 113, 126, 129, 132-134, 155-157, 165-
166, 170, 172, 175, 179, 185, 189, 198-199, 207-208, 212, 217, 225,
234, 242, 251, 255
showing   132
signature   104, 250
signatures   163
signed 243
signers 253
silent   228
similar   28, 33, 58, 68, 155, 183, 194
simple   240
Simply   8
simulator   229
single   101, 257
single-use   7
situation   17, 43, 125, 240
situations   90
skeptical   107
skills   16-17, 57, 102, 118-119, 168, 190, 196, 201, 206, 229-231,
250
smallest   21, 83
Social   1-13, 15-56, 58-70, 72-87, 89-100, 102-142, 144-148, 150-
151, 153-157, 159, 161-163, 165, 167-175, 177-181, 183, 185, 187-
189, 191-203, 205-207, 209-211, 213-217, 219-221, 223, 225-227,
229-231, 233-236, 238, 240-242, 244, 246-251, 253, 255-258
socially 258
societal   103
software   17, 137, 196, 199, 201, 213, 244, 258
solicit   31, 228

solution   48, 66, 69, 73-74, 76-78, 81-82, 84, 88, 244-245
solutions   47, 78, 80-81, 93, 134
solved 16, 136
Someone   7
something   117, 134, 182, 196, 224
Sometimes   47
source 4, 115, 120, 203, 207, 209
sources   38, 58, 70, 168
special 29, 89, 127, 211
specific   8, 22, 29, 36, 39, 103, 125, 144, 147, 156-157, 161,
163, 165, 175, 189-190, 205, 207, 216, 220
specified   121, 150, 249
specify 229
spoken 107
sponsor   23, 135, 145, 174, 213
sponsored   34
sponsors   24, 225, 230
spread 91
stable 139, 195, 202
staffed 34
staffing 16, 96, 146
stages 154, 191
standard   7, 91, 96, 163, 167-168, 244
standards   1, 9-10, 92-95, 146, 181, 185, 220, 232, 238, 250
started 8, 161
starting 9
startup 127
start-up   130
stated 112, 182, 223, 255
statement   3, 10, 80, 83, 137, 144-145, 176
statements   11, 25, 36, 40, 42, 56, 71, 87, 99, 123, 144, 223
static   217
status   5, 65, 136-137, 150, 153-154, 192, 197, 205, 215, 217, 233,
239-240, 244
steady 54
steering   137, 147, 192
storage   185, 224
strategic   46, 74, 90, 118, 174, 209
strategies   75, 98, 107, 120, 211, 221
strategy   16, 38, 55, 74, 82, 86, 97, 100, 104, 116, 121, 132,
208, 212, 221, 239, 255
Stream 62, 64
strengths   146, 246

stretch 106
strict   / 1
strive   106
strong 189
Strongly   10, 15, 27, 43, 57, 73, 88, 100, 217
Structure   3, 78, 102, 148-149, 165, 205, 207
structured   115, 191, 208
structures   132, 237
stubborn   116
stupid 106
subfactor   208
subject8-9, 41
subjects   70
submitted   219
submitting   184
subsequent   208
subset 21
subSocial   199
sub-teams   237
succeed   54, 104
success   16, 18, 29, 32, 37, 40, 44-46, 51, 74, 77, 83, 86, 90,
101, 106, 108, 110, 113, 122, 125, 127, 132, 144, 175, 213, 215,
221, 232, 248, 257
successes   107
successful   75, 94, 112, 114, 126, 128, 165, 167, 180, 215
succession   95, 130
successor   153
suddenly   195
sufficient   224, 231, 234
suggest   201
suggested   89, 219-220
suitable   195, 199
summary   187
supervisor   189
supplier   83, 114
suppliers   38, 59, 62, 119, 154
supplies   246, 251
supply 54
support   7, 20, 66, 94-95, 103, 107, 121, 153, 163, 196-197,
212, 221, 223, 231, 245
supported   68
supporting   89, 186, 209, 224, 251
supportive   192

supports 126
supposed 223
surface 89
SUSTAIN 2, 77, 100
sustained 235
sustaining 90, 159, 227
symptom 15, 44
system 9, 31, 64, 69, 89, 110, 119, 141, 150, 153, 181, 219, 221, 224, 238-241
systematic 50, 150
systems 59-60, 63, 71, 77, 96, 137, 147, 223, 240, 247
tackle 44
tactics 221
taking 52, 216, 239
talent 64, 112
talents 102
talking 7
target 31, 119
targets 106, 241
tasked 98
teaming 228
technical 132, 134, 141, 150, 159, 167-168, 199, 208
techniques 66, 117, 135, 257
technology 49, 80, 91, 122, 127, 133, 140, 168, 227-228
template 171
templates 7-8
tender 251
tenders 250
test-cycle 185
tested 24, 181
testing 147, 181-183, 195, 257
thematic 130
themselves 120, 230
theory 97
therefore 203
therein 151
theyre 138
things 86, 120, 125, 199, 248
thinking 85, 115
thinks 224
third- 74
thorough 82, 179
thought 193

threat 24
threaten   171
threats 204
threshold   181
through   62, 70, 119, 199, 230
throughout   1, 64, 122, 146, 162, 167
tighter 107
time based   187
time-bound   36
timeframe   58, 157, 177
timeframes   22
timeline   173, 184, 219, 234
timely 35, 78, 191, 238-239
Timescales   159
timetable   161, 251
Timing 201, 225
together   122, 250
tolerable   203
tolerances   86, 233
tolerated   155
tomorrow   91, 117
top-down   92
touched   141
toward95, 216
towards   66, 132-133
tracked   195
tracking   37, 90, 146, 173, 182, 205
traction   107
trademark   1
trademarks   1
tradeoff   207-208
trade-offs   192
trained29, 37
training   16, 18-19, 23, 61, 63, 79, 89, 96, 98, 134, 147, 181,
189, 195, 211, 214-215, 224, 231, 243, 257
trainings   19
Transfer   11, 26, 42, 56, 72, 87, 96, 98-99, 123, 244
transition   119, 201
translated   29
trends 66, 68, 85, 112, 182, 203
trigger 75, 86
triggers82, 179, 206
trophy 122

trouble 102
trying   7, 108, 112, 204, 223
turnaround   157
typical 233
ubiquitous   105
unclear   33
underlying   80
undermine   112
understand   40, 66, 138, 172, 189, 228-229, 243
understood   77, 80, 116, 188, 199, 229
undertake   70
undertaken   211
underway   74, 128
uninformed   118
universe   242
Unless 7
unresolved   154, 163
update   256
updated   8-9, 145, 161, 174, 192
updates   9, 96, 244
updating   174
upfront 212
upload 228
usability   118
usable 238
useful 78, 98, 168, 195, 257
usefully 9, 21
utility   169
utilized 242
utilizing 82
validate   240
validated   32, 36, 38, 64
Validation   240
valuable   7
values 92, 119, 130, 182, 203
variables   63, 97
variance   5, 150, 167, 230, 238
-variance   180
variances   136, 167, 174, 187-188, 238-239
variation   15, 39, 58, 70, 95
variety 83
various 154, 191
vendor 73, 174, 210

vendors   20, 64, 74, 137, 154
ventilated   224
verified9, 32, 36, 38, 168
verify   44-45, 48, 51-54, 93, 96, 133, 241, 253
Version 244, 259
versions   27-28
versus 138-139
vested 104
viable 93, 149
vice-versa   255
viewpoint   255
viewpoints   255
vigorously   237
violate 147
violated   146
violations   147
vision   119
visits   210
visualize   155, 170
voices 129
voided 251
volatile 85
volatility   199
volunteer   242
volunteers   227
warranty   1
weaknesses   207, 246
website   228
weighted   167
whether   7, 92, 115
widespread   91
willing 179
windfall   135
window   157
within   70, 84, 155, 157, 170, 203, 215, 220, 247
without1, 11, 101, 122, 140, 153, 220, 250, 253
worked   125, 135, 194, 235
workers   113
workflow   65, 222
workforce   16, 85, 110, 119, 121
workgroup   250
working   92, 94, 132, 189, 195-196, 198, 210, 222
work-life   189

Worksheet   3-4, 169, 177
worksheets   208
worst-case   41
writing 142
written 1, 223, 243, 251
yesterday   19
youhave   138, 171
yourself   105, 108, 116, 189, 213

CPSIA information can be obtained
at www.ICGtesting.com
Printed in the USA
BVHW082019110819
555624BV00016BA/1889/P